It's another Quality Book from CGP

Want to hear the **bad news**? There's an awful lot of heavy stuff you need to know for GCSE separate sciences.

Want to hear the **good news**? Good old CGP have got it all covered! We've produced this brilliant book with all the concepts beautifully explained in clear, simple English so you can understand it — and remember it.

And then, in the spirit of going the extra mile, we've put in a smattering of not-so-serious bits to try and make the whole experience at least partly entertaining for you.

We've done all we can — the rest is up to you.

What CGP is all about

Our sole aim here at CGP is to produce the highest quality books — carefully written, immaculately presented and dangerously close to being funny.

Then we work our socks off to get them out to you — at the cheapest possible prices.

Contents

Published by: Coordination Group Publications Ltd

Contributors: Charley Darbishire
                             James Dawson
                             Sandy Gardner
                             Gemma Hallam
                             Jason Howell
                             Sharon Keeley
                             Tim Major
                             Andy Park
                             Claire Reed
                             Glenn Rogers
                             Rachel Selway
                             Claire Thompson
                             Mike Thompson
                             Luke Waller

ISBN 1-84146-211-X
Groovy Website: www.cgpbooks.co.uk

Printed by Elanders Hindson, Newcastle upon Tyne.
Clipart sources: CorelDRAW and VECTOR.

Pathogens — Bacteria and Viruses

Another day, another exciting new book... And it starts with diseases and stuff. Lovely.

Infectious Diseases are Caused by Pathogens

1) Pathogens are micro-organisms that cause disease and decay.

2) They include some bacteria, protozoa (certain single-celled creatures) and fungi, and all viruses.

3) All pathogens are parasites — they live off their host and give nothing in return.

4) Micro-organisms can reproduce very fast inside a host organism.

Louis Pasteur found Evidence that Living Organisms cause Disease and Decay

1) Pasteur used flasks of broth, which had been boiled so that any micro-organisms in the broth would be killed off.

2) One flask had an S-shaped neck plugged with cotton wool — so fresh air could get in, but any micro-organisms in the air would not reach the broth. The other flask had a straight neck, which was left open.

3) The broth in the flask with the S-shaped neck did not go mouldy and cloudy, but the broth in a control flask with a straight neck did go cloudy.

4) The conclusion was that things went off and decayed because of living organisms in the air. Before these experiments people had thought that mould and bacteria magically appeared from nowhere when things went off. Fools.

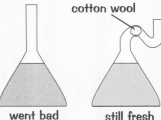

cotton wool

went bad   still fresh

Bacteria are Single Cells with No Nucleus

1) Bacteria reproduce by dividing in two by mitosis to form two new cells.

2) Reproducing bacteria form visible colonies on a petri dish of agar jelly. Bacteria growing in a flask of clear broth turn the clear broth cloudy. You can see how quickly the bacteria are reproducing by measuring how the area of the colonies, or the cloudiness of the liquid, changes with time.

3) Some bacteria form tough spores when life gets hard.

4) Bacterial spores are resistant to heat, cold, drying out, pH change and the effects of some chemicals. Tough little blighters, eh.

5) When conditions get more favourable for the little bacteria to live and reproduce, the spores "wake up" and grow into new bacterial cells.

6) Whooping cough and tetanus are examples of diseases caused by bacteria.

cell membrane

cell wall

cytoplasm

chromosome (nucleoid) — just one, free-floating in the cytoplasm

sometimes also contain plasmids (DNA that isn't part of the main chromosome)

Viruses Invade Cells

1) Viruses are just a strand of DNA or RNA inside a protein coat. They're not cells, and they don't have all the basic processes that most organisms have.

2) They reproduce by injecting their DNA (or RNA) into a host cell. The poor host cell can't help using the virus DNA (or RNA) to make virus proteins.

3) The virus proteins assemble into new viruses, and burst out of the cell when the time's right (generally destroying the cell in the process).

4) The common cold is caused by a virus.

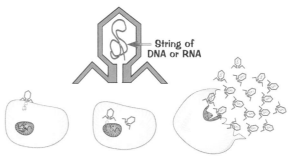

String of DNA or RNA

Who feels like a nice hot cup of broth then...

Mmm... tasty...

Pathogens — Fungi and Yeast

You need to know all about yeast and fungi, and how they reproduce. Try not to get squeemish now...

Fungi and Moulds have Branching Hyphae

This is what fungi look like close up:

Diseases caused by fungi include athlete's foot and thrush. Fungi reproduce either by producing spores, or by budding.

Mould is somewhere between a single-celled organism and a multi-celled organism.
Moulds also consist of branching structures (called hyphae) — like those in fungi. Hyphae aren't divided into separate cells — the same cytoplasm flows all the way through them, although there are lots of nuclei.
Moulds can be useful in industry and medicine — penicillin comes from a mould, for example.

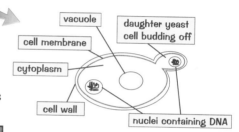

a mycelium — made up of loads of...
...hyphae
hyphal membrane
hyphal wall
nuclei
cytoplasm

Yeast is a Single-Celled Fungus

Yeast reproduces asexually by budding — as the diagram shows:
Learn the equation for anaerobic respiration (i.e. without oxygen) of glucose by yeast (this process is called fermentation):

glucose → ethanol + carbon dioxide + energy

Yeast can also respire aerobically (i.e. with oxygen). This produces much more energy, and is needed to grow and reproduce.

glucose + oxygen → carbon dioxide + water + energy

vacuole
daughter yeast cell budding off
cell membrane
cytoplasm
cell wall
nuclei containing DNA

The Rate of Bacterial/Fungal Reproduction Varies

In the Exam, you might have to explain bacterial/fungal population data.

1) Bacteria and fungi reproduce faster when it's warmer, but if it's too hot they die.

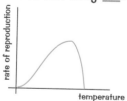

rate of reproduction / temperature

2) The more food there is, the faster they reproduce.

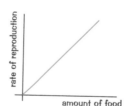

rate of reproduction / amount of food

3) Build-up of toxic waste products slows reproduction down.

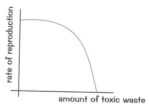

rate of reproduction / amount of toxic waste

There are Loads of Ways Infectious Diseases can Spread

1) Some diseases are spread by pathogens that live in water, e.g. cholera bacteria.
2) Pathogens can also live and reproduce in food — e.g. the bacteria salmonella and listeria.
3) The influenza (flu) and the common cold viruses are spread through the air.
4) Some diseases are spread by direct or indirect contact, e.g. the athlete's foot fungus.
5) The hepatitis B virus is spread through body fluids, e.g. blood and semen.
6) Some pathogens enter the body via another animal. A disease caused in this way is non-infectious — the disease is not spread from one person to another. Houseflies can carry the dysentery bacterium. The protozoan which causes malaria is carried by a mosquito, and enters the blood when the mosquito bites to suck blood. An animal which carries and spreads a pathogen is called a disease vector.

Any budding mycologists out there...

So if athletes would just quit running and stick their feet in some ice, they'd be fine. I've no sympathy.

The Spread of Disease

A couple of hundred years ago, it was virtually unheard of for someone in Britain to catch malaria. But nowadays it's dead easy to travel — you can just nip over to Africa for a holiday, and wham. Malaria.

Controlling the Spread of Malaria, Flu and AIDS

1) Malaria is caused by a protozoan. The *Anopheles* mosquito carries the protozoan, and spreads it through its bite. Malaria is endemic to tropical Africa.

2) The symptoms of malaria are fever, chills and shaking.

3) The spread of malaria is controlled by controlling the population of the *Anopheles* mosquito — usually by using insecticides.

Endemic means the disease is always in a particular area.

Epidemic means the disease has been brought in from elsewhere.

1) Flu, or influenza, to give it its proper name, is caused by a virus. The virus is spread through the air — infected droplets of water from an infected person's cough or sneeze are breathed in by someone else.

2) The symptoms of flu are fever, aching muscles and a runny nose.

3) Flu is dangerous to the old and weak. Older people are offered a vaccination against flu each year.

1) Aquired Immune Deficiency Syndrome (AIDS) is caused by the Human Immunodeficiency Virus (HIV). HIV is only spread by body fluids being exchanged between an infected person and someone else. Unprotected sexual intercourse and sharing needles for injection (without disinfecting them) are the main ways that HIV spreads.

2) AIDS causes the immune system to break down. The body of an AIDS sufferer has difficulty fighting off disease.

3) The spread of HIV is fought mainly by education. People are taught safer sexual practices, like always using a condom. Needle exchange programmes are sometimes set up for drug addicts.

Good Hygiene Reduces the Spread of Disease

1) Clean water and proper plumbing is really important. Good sanitation means that bacteria from human faeces can't get into the drinking water. Before towns had clean water, diseases like cholera were common.

2) Diseases like the common cold are spread mainly by people sneezing near each other. People with a cold can help stop spreading it by staying at home when they're ill.

3) Good foot hygiene stops athlete's foot from getting passed on, e.g. covering the infected foot while swimming etc.

4) Tapeworm eggs are passed out in the faeces of an infected person. Pigs or cows kept on soil contaminated with human waste can ingest the eggs and carry the larvae in their muscles. When they're killed and eaten, especially if they're not well cooked, the parasite can be passed on to humans again.

5) Toxocara is a parasitic worm found in dog and cat faeces. It can cause blindness if it gets in the eyes, so use a poop scoop.

6) Headlice are spread from one head to another through touching. Treating headlice with medicated lotion/shampoo gets rid of them before they have a chance to be passed on to the next person.

Socioeconomic Factors can have a Big Effect

Here's a favourite exam topic for you. Best learn all these other factors too...

1) Nutrition can make a massive difference to how well a person is able to fight off disease.

2) Poor housing can lead to general ill health, due to things like damp, mould, cold, dirt, dust...

3) Living in overcrowded conditions means more contact with people — one person gets ill, so does everyone else.

4) War can contribute to all of these things — fleeing refugees often end up having to live in overcrowded, unsanitary conditions, often with a shortage of food and medical supplies.

5) Education can help make people more aware of how diseases are spread. Poorly educated people may not realise the dangers of, say, drinking dirty water or having unprotected sex.

Get rid of athlete's foot — an axe ought to do it...

Yeuch — loads of nasty diseases. For your exam (and life), you need to learn how all these diseases are transmitted, and how they're prevented. Cleanliness is the key. Look at your hands, they're filthy...

Making Stuff Safer

Pathogens seem to get everywhere — so we've got to have ways of getting rid of them. Fascinating stuff.

Heat, Chemicals and Radiation Kill Pathogens

1) Milk is pasteurised to kill pathogens. The milk is heated to 72 °C for 15 seconds and then quickly cooled down to 3 °C. The heat kills most pathogens, and the quick cooling means that any bacteria that do survive don't have the chance to reproduce before it gets too cold for them. (This is sometimes called the 'flash' process.)

2) Disinfectants, e.g. bleach and toilet cleaner, are chemicals used to kill micro-organisms. Chlorine is used to disinfect water in swimming pools.

3) Antiseptics, e.g. TCP and Savlon, are used on the body itself, e.g. on a wound, or as a throat spray. Most disinfectants are far too toxic to be used directly on the body.

4) Radiation is also used to kill pathogens. Some food is irradiated to kill bacteria, fungi and other pathogens. However, there's a danger that the food may still contain some of their toxins.

Tap Water is Treated to make it Safe

1) The water is left to stand while large dirt particles settle and form a sediment — this is sedimentation.

2) Smaller particles, including pathogens, are filtered out by passing the water through beds of sand.

3) Chlorine is added to kill any micro-organisms still in the water.

Sewage is Treated with an 'Activated Sludge' of Bacteria

If untreated sewage is dumped into a river, it'll starve the water of oxygen, killing plants and fish and creating a nasty health risk. The river can't then be used for water supply, fishing, boating or swimming.

Sewage includes everything that goes down the drain — washing-up water, bathwater and anything you chuck down the sink or loo. It's not just urine and faeces.

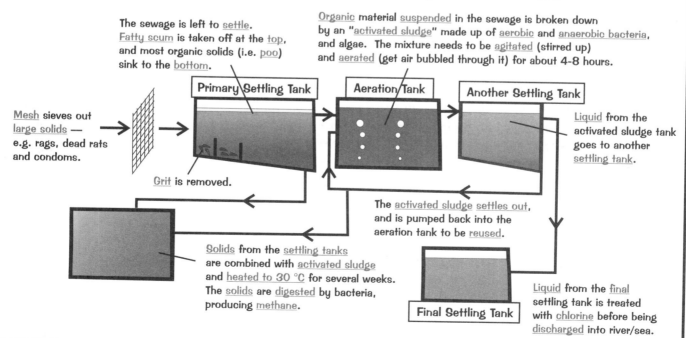

The sewage is left to settle. Fatty scum is taken off at the top, and most organic solids (i.e. poo) sink to the bottom.

Organic material suspended in the sewage is broken down by an "activated sludge" made up of aerobic and anaerobic bacteria, and algae. The mixture needs to be agitated (stirred up) and aerated (get air bubbled through it) for about 4-8 hours.

Mesh sieves out large solids — e.g. rags, dead rats and condoms.

Primary Settling Tank

Aeration Tank

Another Settling Tank

Liquid from the activated sludge tank goes to another settling tank.

Grit is removed.

The activated sludge settles out, and is pumped back into the aeration tank to be reused.

Solids from the settling tanks are combined with activated sludge and heated to 30 °C for several weeks. The solids are digested by bacteria, producing methane.

Final Settling Tank

Liquid from the final settling tank is treated with chlorine before being discharged into river/sea.

I hate learning about sewage — it's a load of cr...

Actually, I never knew a sewage works could be so fascinating. It's not something you really think about, until you have to learn it for GCSE. Which would be about now — so get learning.

Food Poisoning

Food poisoning — not pleasant and easy to avoid. Worth reading even if you're hacked off with revision.

Food Poisoning can be Caused by Bacteria

1) Food poisoning can be caused by <u>various bacteria</u>, including <u>salmonella</u> and <u>Escherichia coli</u> (E. coli).

2) <u>Salmonella</u> is carried by <u>chickens</u>, and found in chicken meat and eggs.

3) Salmonella bacteria produce <u>toxins</u> which damage the <u>gut</u>, and cause <u>pain</u>, <u>diarrhoea</u> and <u>vomiting</u>.

4) If meat and eggs are stored in <u>warm conditions</u>, any salmonella bacteria present <u>reproduce very fast</u>.

Normal cow   Mad cow

Good farming practices also help prevent food poisoning.

Look at BSE and vCJD, for example ("mad cow disease" and the human equivalent). Feeding cow brains and spinal cords to other cows is bound to cause problems.

Good Kitchen Hygiene Helps Prevent Food Poisoning

1) Food must be stored at a <u>cool temperature</u>. Remember, "warmth = bacteria reproducing like mad".

2) <u>Uncooked meat</u> must not be allowed to contaminate <u>cooked food</u>, or food that's <u>eaten raw</u>. Uncooked meat should always be stored on a <u>low shelf</u> in the fridge, otherwise juices might <u>drip onto other food</u>. Eeeewwww...

3) <u>Hands must be washed</u> before preparing food. And that means <u>washed properly</u>, in <u>hot soapy water</u>.

4) After handling <u>uncooked meat</u>, hands must be <u>washed in hot soapy water</u>. <u>Utensils</u> used with uncooked meat or fish must <u>not be used</u> to prepare <u>other foods</u> without being washed properly first.

5) Using <u>separate chopping boards</u> for meat, fish, veg and dairy stuff reduces the risk of contamination.

6) <u>Cooking eggs thoroughly</u>, and <u>avoiding foods</u> containing <u>uncooked eggs</u> (e.g. home-made mayonnaise), reduces the risk of salmonella poisoning.

Food is Preserved to stop it Going Bad

1) Food can be preserved by <u>canning</u> — the airtight can keeps micro-organisms from getting into food. The food is also <u>heated in the can</u> to kill any micro-organisms that are already there.

2) <u>Frozen food</u> won't go bad as quickly — micro-organisms can't grow and reproduce if it's too cold (although they're not actually <u>killed</u> by freezing).

3) Some food is preserved by <u>drying</u> — micro-organisms need water for life processes. Removing water stops them from growing and reproducing.

4) <u>Ultra heat treatment</u> means heating food to high temperatures for a short time to kill micro-organisms. UHT milk is milk that's been heated to 132 °C for 1 second.

It keeps for months, but doesn't taste the same as ordinary pasteurised milk.

5) Food can be preserved by <u>salting</u> — a high concentration of salt makes bacteria "pop" due to <u>osmosis</u>. Remember your definition of osmosis — *water moves from a less concentrated solution to a more concentrated solution through a differentially permeable membrane*, e.g. cell membrane. Preserving food in a <u>concentrated sugar solution</u> (e.g. <u>jam</u>, candied fruit) works in the same way.

Mmm... sun-dried tomatoes...

6) Food can be preserved by <u>pickling in vinegar</u>. Most pathogens can't survive <u>low pH</u>.

It was the salmon mousse I tell you...

This page is full of common-sense stuff really. Make sure you learn all the different ways of <u>preserving food</u>. You never know when you'll get asked about them. If you've learnt it all *properly*, you should be able to write down all the <u>subheadings</u>, and all the <u>main points</u>.

Defence Against Disease

There's one almighty battle going on each time a "nasty" tries to infect you. It's fascinating stuff...

White Blood Cells Defend the Body against Pathogens

Phagocytes can engulf microbes (i.e. micro-organisms) and digest them.

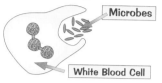

Microbes

White Blood Cell

Lymphocytes produce antibodies as part of the immune system.

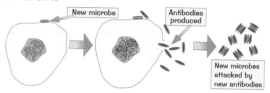

New microbe

Antibodies produced

New microbes attacked by new antibodies

B- and T-type Lymphocytes make up the Immune Response

1) T-cells have receptors on their surface that recognise particular antigens (antigen is a fancy Biology word for any substance (e.g. a pathogen) that triggers a response from the body's immune system).

2) T-cells attach to a particular antigen and then destroy the cell which has that antigen.

3) B-cells secrete antibodies, which are specific to a particular antigen. Once a T-cell has spotted an antigen, it gives a signal to B-cells to multiply and make a big population of identical cells to secrete lots of identical antibodies to fight the infection.

4) Memory B-cells stay around in the blood after the original infection has been fought. They can reproduce very fast if the same antigen enters the body for a second time. That's why you're immune to most diseases if you've already had them — the body carries a "memory" of what the antigen was like, so it can produce loads of antibodies to bash the infection just like that if you get infected again.

5) Another antibody fact to learn — breast milk contains antibodies, to make the baby pre-immune to some diseases. Clever old thing, Nature...

Vaccination protects against Viruses

1) Vaccination involves injecting dead or weakened virus material into the body. The body's lymphocytes react by producing antibodies.

2) If live viruses infect the body later on, they're blatted immediately. The body "remembers" antibodies it's made before. Memory B-cells trigger speedy production of antibodies to destroy the viruses.

3) In the UK, vaccinations are often given to children at a young age, e.g. the MMR (Measles, Mumps and Rubella) vaccine that there's been a bit of publicity about recently.

4) If someone is infected with a dangerous pathogen, e.g. some types of rabies, ready-made antibodies are injected to combat the infection straight away.

Well don't look at us...

Monoclonal Antibodies are lots of Identical Antibodies

One way of making lots of identical antibodies is to use mouse lymphocytes:

1) A mouse is injected with an antigen, and some of the antibody-producing lymphocytes it produces are removed.

2) One of these lymphocytes is fused with a tumour cell, and the hybrid cell is left to reproduce.

3) Tumour cells are used because they divide like crazy, giving a large colony of identical (clone) cells in a short time. The colony of cells produces identical antibodies, which are harvested.

4) Monoclonal antibodies are used for treating disease, and also for detecting the specific antigen that they fit on to.

White blood cells — great album...

There are a lot of big words on this page, but the main things to learn are the processes involved. You need to know how white blood cells defend against pathogens, how antigens are recognised and stopped, and how immunisation works — it's tricky stuff, but really quite interesting if you think about it.

Antibiotics

Antibiotics are brilliant, but they're easy to overuse. I watched 'Outbreak' the other day. Worrying...

Antibiotics Kill Bacteria

Antibiotics kill bacteria inside the body. They actually <u>cure</u> the disease by <u>getting rid of the infection</u>, unlike many other medicines that only cure the <u>symptoms</u> (e.g. painkillers).

<u>Antibiotics can't kill viruses</u>. Viruses live and reproduce <u>inside the body's cells</u>. It'd be very hard to kill the viruses without damaging the body's own cells as well.

Penicillin Comes from a Fungus

1) Various types of *Penicillium* fungus produce <u>natural antibiotics</u> called <u>penicillins</u>.

2) <u>Penicillins</u> kill bacteria by stopping them from making a cell wall.

3) Penicillins are produced on an industrial scale in <u>huge fermenters</u>, like the one in the diagram.

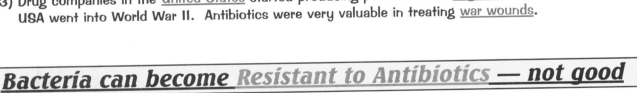

Food and water in

Exhaust gases/water vapour out

Penicillium in

Coolant out

Coolant in

Paddles to stir the mixture

Air in

Product (penicillin) out

...and was discovered by Fleming

1) Penicillin was first discovered by <u>Alexander Fleming</u>, who noticed that bacteria did not grow near *Penicillium* mould.

2) Penicillin was not produced until the <u>1940s</u>, when <u>Howard Florey</u>, <u>Ernst Chain</u> and their Oxford research team found a way to purify it enough for use on humans.

3) Drug companies in the <u>United States</u> started producing penicillin on a <u>large scale</u> in <u>1941</u> — when the USA went into World War II. Antibiotics were very valuable in treating <u>war wounds</u>.

Bacteria can become Resistant to Antibiotics — not good

1) Bacteria <u>evolve</u> antibiotic resistance by <u>natural selection</u>. If one bacterium is resistant to an antibiotic, it's likely to survive and pass the resistance gene on to the next generation.

2) Doctors need a <u>wide range</u> of antibiotics to choose from, so that they can pick a suitable antibiotic that will <u>actually kill</u> all the bacteria they're trying to get rid of.

3) The risk of bacteria getting resistant to antibiotics is <u>increased</u> by:
— doctors giving patients antibiotics when they <u>don't need them</u>,
— patients <u>not taking all</u> the antibiotics they're given when they do need them.
(It's important to <u>finish</u> a course of antibiotics because otherwise some bacteria may survive, and become resistant.)

4) Lots of <u>research</u> needs to be done all the time to develop <u>new drugs</u> that the bacteria aren't resistant to yet.

Just have your tonsils out — much safer...*

Eeek — scary thought. All the time we're developing <u>new</u> antibiotics, and bacteria are <u>evolving</u> and getting <u>resistant</u> to them, so we need new antibiotics, which they'll then become resistant to... and so it goes on. I guess at the end of the day, things just find a way to <u>survive</u>. Darn.

* ...er ...so then you can get tracheitis, laryngitis or bronchitis instead of tonsillitis. Hmm.

The Blood, the Brain and Reflexes

Blood, brain and reflexes — pretty important for keeping us alive, I'd say. And for your GCSE Biology.

The ABO Blood Group System is all about Antibodies

1) People have different blood groups — you can be any one of: A, B, O and AB.
2) Red blood cells can have A or B antigens on their surface, and the blood plasma can contain anti-A or anti-B antibodies.
3) If an anti-A antibody meets an A antigen, the blood clots up and it all goes hideously wrong. Same thing when an anti-B antibody meets a B antigen.
4) So... this means that some blood groups can't get blood transfusions from other blood groups. The table makes it crystal clear:

Blood Group	Antigens	Antibodies	Can give blood to	Can get blood from
A	A	anti-B	A and AB	A and O
B	B	anti-A	B and AB	B and O
AB	A, B	none	only AB	anyone
O	none	anti-A, anti-B	anyone	only O

For example, 'O blood' can be given to anyone — there are no antigens on the blood cells, so any anti-A or anti-B antibodies have nothing to 'attack'.

High Blood Pressure can cause a Stroke

Other stuff you need to know about the blood — blood pressure. It's dead important to keep a constant healthy blood pressure. The kidneys need it for ultrafiltration of blood, for a start (see the Double Science Biology book). And the brain needs constant blood pressure too. If it gets too high, there's a risk of a stroke — burst blood vessels in the brain, which can damage the soft sensitive brain tissue, causing such problems as paralysis, speech problems, memory loss and death.

The Brain is Full of Exciting Stuff — and Biology Facts

Cerebellum — controls the sense of balance and position. Automatic movements to balance yourself or stop yourself falling over come from the cerebellum.

Cerebrum — collects sensory information from sense receptors, controls voluntary actions, and is where conscious thought happens, and memory is stored.

Spinal cord — where sensory neurone meets motor neurone in a reflex arc (see below).

Medulla — controls certain reflex actions, such as heart rate and breathing rate.

The Reflex Arc — a Few Picky Details...

The reflex arc is covered in the Double Science Biology Book.
But if you're doing OCR GCSE Biology, you also need to know these few extra details:

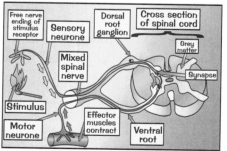

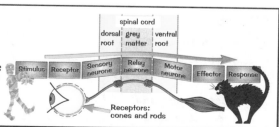

This diagram shows the order that things happen in a reflex arc. Note when the message passes through each of the bits of the spinal cord.

Blood and brains — the very best of Black Pudding...

Get that blood group table learnt. If you think you can leave it until the Exam, and somehow figure it all out then — well, sorry, but you're wrong. Other than that, there's not too much to learn here. Scribble down a quick version of the brain diagram, and practise matching names to the right squishy bits.

Kidney Disease

Oh great, another page on illness. Fantastic.

The Kidneys Remove Toxic Substances from the Blood

1) If the kidneys don't work properly, toxic substances build up in the blood. Eventually, this results in death.

2) People with kidney disease can be kept alive and healthy by having dialysis treatment — where machines do the job of removing waste from the blood.

> The kidneys are incredibly important — if they don't work as they should, you can get problems in the heart, bones, nervous system, stomach, mouth, etc.

Dialysis Machines Filter the Blood

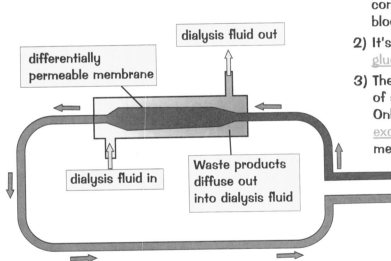

differentially permeable membrane

dialysis fluid out

dialysis fluid in

Waste products diffuse out into dialysis fluid

from person

back to person

1) Dialysis has to be done regularly to keep the concentration of dissolved substances in the blood at normal levels.

2) It's important not to lose mineral salts and glucose from the blood during dialysis.

3) The dialysis fluid has the same concentration of salts and glucose as healthy blood plasma. Only waste substances (such as urea) and excess ions and water move across the membrane.

Organ Transplants can be Rejected by the Body

At the moment, the only cure for kidney disease is to have a kidney transplant. Healthy kidneys are usually transplanted from people who have died suddenly, say in a car accident, and who are on the organ donor register or carry a donor card (provided their relatives give the go-ahead). But kidneys can also be transplanted from people who are still alive.

The donor kidney can be rejected by the patient's immune system — treated like a foreign body and attacked by antibodies. To prevent this happening, precautions are taken:

1) A donor with a tissue type that matches the patient is chosen.

2) The patient's bone marrow is zapped with radiation to stop white blood cells being produced.

3) The patient is treated with drugs that almost completely stop the immune system response. Unfortunately, this also means that the patient can't fight any disease that comes along, so they have to be kept in totally sterile conditions after the operation.

N.B. Sometimes a blood transfusion is necessary during the transplant operation — this must be of a compatible blood group (see page 8).

Dialysis does this automatically — you have to LEARN it...

Kidney dialysis machines are expensive things for the NHS to run — and dialysis is not a pleasant experience. But it's the only choice some people have got — if a transplant isn't possible for whatever reason, they're pretty much stuck with it. But on the plus side, at least there are dialysis machines.

Revision Summary for Section One

Wow. That's one heck of a section to start off with. Dead interesting, like, but there's some real tricky stuff in there and you've GOT TO LEARN IT. If you don't bother, you'll be throwing marks away and resigning yourself to a lower grade in the exam. You've got the book, so you may as well use it.

These questions are designed to <u>really test</u> whether you know your stuff — ignore them at your peril. <u>Yes</u>, they <u>are</u> difficult. But the information's all in the section, so if you get bits wrong, go back, look it up and try again.

It's no use just reading through and thinking you've got it all — it'll only stick if you've learnt it <u>properly</u>. OK, rant over — I'll leave you to it...

1) What is a pathogen?
2) Are all bacteria pathogens?
3) Do bacteria have a nucleus?
4) How do bacteria reproduce?
5) Describe in detail how viruses invade cells.
6) In what two ways do fungi reproduce?
7) Draw a diagram of a branching mycelium, with a detailed diagram of one of the hyphae.
8) Is yeast a single-celled or a multiple-celled organism?
9) Give an example of a disease that is spread through contaminated water.
10) Give an example of a human disease that is carried by other animals.
11) What is the term for an animal which carries and spreads disease?
12) How are people trying to control the spread of AIDS?
13) Describe 4 ways in which good hygiene can reduce the spread of disease.
14) Describe how wars can increase the risk of disease spreading.
15) In the flash pasteurisation process, how hot is milk heated, and for how long?
16) Give an example of a disinfectant and an example of an antiseptic. What's the difference?
17) What is activated sludge, and what does it do in the sewage treatment process?
18) How does salmonella damage the body?
19) Give four examples of how good kitchen hygiene prevents food poisoning.
20) Say how each of these preserving methods stops food going bad:
    a) freezing, b) canning, c) ultra heat treatment.
21) What is the role of T-cells in the immune response?
22) What is the role of memory B-cells in the immune response?
23) Describe what vaccination is, and why it works.
24) What are monoclonal antibodies, and how can they be produced?
25) How is penicillin made commercially?
26) Why is it important to finish a course of antibiotics prescribed by a doctor?
27) Which antigens and antibodies are present in the blood of someone with group A blood?
28) Name two organs that need a constant healthy blood pressure to function properly.
29) What is the role of the cerebellum?
30) How does kidney dialysis work?
31) Why do transplant patients have their immune systems suppressed?

Growing Micro-organisms

Micro-organisms can be grown in a lab, but they need certain conditions to flourish.
Also, precautions must be taken to stop unwanted micro-organisms growing as well.

Micro-organisms are grown on Agar Jelly in a Petri Dish

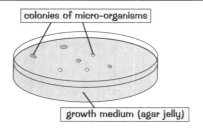

colonies of micro-organisms

growth medium (agar jelly)

1) Micro-organisms are grown (cultured) in a "culture medium".
2) They need carbohydrates as an energy source, plus mineral ions, and sometimes supplementary proteins and vitamins.
3) These nutrients are usually contained in agar jelly.
4) Agar jelly can be poured when hot, and sets when cold. It's poured into shallow round plastic dishes called petri dishes.

Equipment is Sterilised to Prevent Contamination

1) If equipment isn't sterilised, unwanted micro-organisms in the growth medium will grow and contaminate the end product.
2) The unwanted micro-organisms might make harmful substances, or cause disease.
3) Petri dishes and the growth medium must be sterilised before use.
4) Inoculating loops (used for transferring micro-organisms to the growth medium) are sterilised by passing them through a flame.
5) The petri dish must have a lid to stop any micro-organisms in the air contaminating the culture. The lid should be taped on.

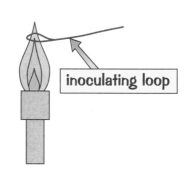

inoculating loop

Pathogens are micro-organisms which cause disease. See Section 1 for more info.

In the lab at school, cultures of micro-organisms are kept at about 25 °C. This is not warm enough for harmful pathogens to grow. In industrial conditions, cultures are incubated at higher temperatures so that they can grow a lot faster.

Advantages of Micro-organisms for Food Production

Micro-organisms can be grown to produce food and drink. Yum — tasty.

1) Micro-organisms like bacteria and fungi grow very quickly.
2) They're also easy to look after. All that's needed is something to grow them in, food, oxygen, and the right temperature.
3) Another plus is that it'll mean that food can be produced whether the climate is hot or cold.
4) Micro-organisms can use waste products from agriculture and industry as fuel for their life processes.

1) Mycoprotein means protein from fungi.
2) Mycoprotein is used in the food industry. It's used to make meat substitutes for vegetarian meals — Quorn, for example.
3) A fungus called *Fusarium* is the main source of mycoprotein.

Invite mushrooms to parties — they're fun guys...

Growth medium = culture medium = liquid or jelly that the micro-organisms are grown in. Sorted.
Make sure you learn all the advantages of using micro-organisms in food production. The best way to do that is to jot them all down without looking back at the page. Keep on going until you can.

Micro-organisms in Food Production

This page is enough to put you off cheese for life. Especially the smelly blue stuff.

Cheese _is made by_ Bacteria

You need to know how cheese is made, so here goes...

1) A culture of bacteria is added to warm milk.

2) The bacteria produce solid curds in the milk.

3) The curds are separated from the liquid whey.

4) More bacteria is added to the curds, and the whole lot is left to ripen for a while.

5) Moulds are added to give blue cheese (e.g. Stilton) its colour and taste.

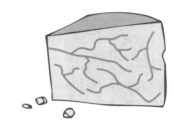

Yeast _is used to make_ Alcoholic Drinks

1) Beer is made from grain — usually barley.

2) The barley grains are allowed to germinate for a few days, and then they're dried in a kiln. The starch in the grains is broken down into sugar by enzymes. This process is called malting.

3) The sugary malt solution is fermented by yeast. The sugar is turned into alcohol.

4) Hops are added to the mixture to give the beer its bitter flavour.

Germination is when a seed starts to grow into a new plant.

Soy Sauce — Fermentation using Fungi _and_ Bacteria

There are different kinds of soy sauce, but they're generally more complicated to make than beer or cheese. This is the process behind one particular kind of soy sauce — it involves different kinds of micro-organism.

1) Cooked soy beans and roasted wheat (or sometimes barley) are mixed together.

2) The mixture is fermented by the Aspergillus fungus.

3) The mixture is fermented again by yeasts.

4) The mixture is fermented yet again by the Lactobacillus bacterium.

5) The liquid is filtered to remove any gungy bits.

6) Then it's pasteurised to kill off the micro-organisms.

7) The sauce is then put into sterile bottles.

Micro-organisms can also cause Food Poisoning

See also Section 1.

1) Micro-organisms aren't always good news.

2) Micro-organisms can contaminate food, causing food poisoning.

3) The chance of food poisoning is reduced by following safety rules for storing, handling and cooking food.

E.g. | Keep raw meat away from cooked meat. | Wash hands before touching food. | Cook meat thoroughly.

A milk and bacteria sandwich anyone?...

You have to know what micro-organisms are involved in the production of each of these foods and drinks. Remember that when it's an alcoholic drink, fermentation by yeast is going to be involved. Soy sauce is quite complicated — don't pretend you've learnt it when you haven't.

Micro-organisms in Industry

In industry, they don't mess around with little petri dishes — or even big petri dishes. They grow shed loads of micro-organisms in huge vats called fermenters to produce things like <u>antibiotics</u>, <u>fuels</u> and <u>proteins</u>.

Micro-organisms are Grown in <u>Fermenters</u> on a <u>Large</u> Scale

A fermenter is a big container full of <u>liquid</u> culture medium which micro-organisms can <u>grow</u> and <u>reproduce</u> in. The fermenter needs to give the micro-organisms the <u>conditions</u> they need to <u>grow</u> and produce their <u>useful product</u>.

1) <u>Food</u> is provided in the liquid culture medium. More can be pumped in if needed.

2) Air is piped in to supply <u>oxygen</u> to the micro-organisms.

3) The micro-organisms need to be kept at the <u>right temperature</u>. The micro-organisms produce <u>heat</u> by respiration, so the fermenters must be <u>cooled</u>. This is usually done with <u>water</u>.

4) The <u>right pH</u> is needed for the micro-organisms to thrive. Instruments will monitor this.

5) <u>Sterile conditions</u> are needed to <u>prevent contamination</u> from other micro-organisms.

6) The micro-organisms need to be kept from <u>sinking to the bottom</u>. A <u>motorised stirrer</u> keeps them moving around and maintains an even temperature.

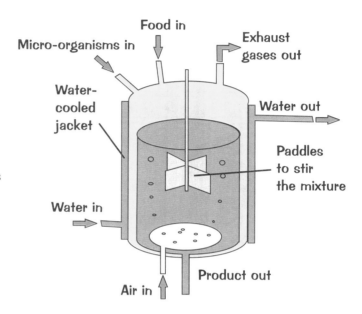

Food from Fermenters — <u>Single-Cell Protein</u>

1) Single-cell protein is made up of the cells of <u>bacteria</u>, <u>fungi</u> or <u>algae</u>. These can be cultured in <u>fermenters</u>.

2) <u>Population growth</u> in <u>developing countries</u> means that soon some countries may not be able to feed themselves. It can be especially <u>difficult</u> to find enough <u>protein</u>. <u>Meat</u> is a big source of protein, but animals need lots of <u>space to graze</u>, plenty of <u>nice grass</u>, etc.

3) <u>Single-cell proteins</u> grown in a fermenter would be an <u>efficient</u> way of producing protein to feed people. <u>Single-celled micro-organisms</u> grow <u>very quickly</u>, and don't need a lot of <u>space</u> to grow. They can <u>feed</u> on <u>waste material</u> that would be no good for feeding animals.

<u>Penicillin</u> is made by Growing Mould in <u>Fermenters</u>

1) <u>Penicillin</u> is an antibiotic made by growing the <u>mould</u> Penicillium in a fermenter.

2) The Penicillium is grown in a liquid culture medium containing <u>sugar</u> and other nutrients.

3) The sugar is used up as the Penicillium grows.

4) The Penicillium only starts to make penicillin after using up <u>most</u> of the nutrients for <u>growth</u>.

Culture Medium — sounds very BBC Four to me...

Once you've <u>learnt this page properly</u>, you should be able to <u>sketch out</u> and <u>label</u> a diagram of a fermenter, and you should know what <u>conditions</u> the micro-organisms need to thrive happily. Go on then — cover the page up and give it a bash. It may seem harsh now, but you'll thank me in the end.

Fuels from Micro-organisms

You only need to learn the things on this page if you're doing the AQA syllabus. The rest of you can just read it for the sheer enjoyment of it. The fun just goes on and on...

Fuels can be made by Fermentation

1) Fuels can be made by fermentation of natural products — luckily enough, waste products can often be used.

2) Fermentation is when bacteria or yeast break sugars down by anaerobic respiration.

> Anaerobic respiration does not use oxygen.

Ethanol is made by Anaerobic Fermentation of Sugar

1) Yeast makes ethanol from glucose (waste from sugar refineries can be used, or glucose can be derived from maize starch by the action of carbohydrase).

> Glucose → Ethanol + Carbon dioxide + Energy

2) In some countries, e.g. Brazil, cars are adapted to run on a mixture of ethanol and petrol — this is known as 'gasohol'.

Biogas is made by Anaerobic Fermentation of Waste Material

1) Biogas is about 70% methane (CH_4) and 30% carbon dioxide (CO_2).

2) Lots of different micro-organisms are used to produce biogas.

3) Biogas is made from plant and animal waste in a simple fermenter called a digester. Sludge waste from, e.g. sewage works (see page 4) or sugar factories, is used to make biogas on a large scale.

4) Biogas digesters need to be kept at a constant temperature to keep the micro-organisms respiring away.

5) There are two types of biogas digesters —

> Batch digesters make biogas in small batches. They're manually loaded up with waste, which is left to digest, and the by-products are cleared away at the end of each session.

> Continuous digesters make biogas all the time. Waste is continuously fed in, and biogas is produced at a steady rate. Continuous digesters are more suited to large-scale biogas projects.

6) Biogas can't be stored as a liquid, so it has to be used straight away — for heating, cooking, lighting, or to power a turbine to generate electricity.

Fuel Production Can Happen on a Small Scale

1) In some (less-developed) countries, small biogas generators are used to make enough gas for a village or a family to use in their cooking stoves.

2) Human waste, waste from keeping pigs and waste from rubbish can be digested by bacteria to produce the biogas.

3) By-products are used to fertilise crops and gardens.

Anaerobics lesson — keep fit for bacteria...

Fascinating stuff, this biogas. It makes a lot of sense, I suppose, to get energy from rubbish, sewage and pig poop instead of leaving it all to rot naturally — which would mean all that lovely methane just wafting away into the atmosphere. Remember — anaerobic respiration makes biofuels.

Manipulating Reproduction

This page is all about breeding livestock on a large scale, and cloning as well. Read on...

Cattle Reproduction *is 'helped along' Artificially*

Gone are the days when a bull and a cow met, fell in love, and decided to start a family. These days, artificial insemination is often used.

1) Sperm is collected from the prize bull. This is done by encouraging him to get 'romantic' with a fake cow, inside which is a container for collecting the semen.

2) The bull semen is diluted to make it go further.

3) It's frozen, and stored.

4) The prize cow is given hormones to make her ovulate.

5) Her eggs are collected.

6) The egg from the prize cow is fertilised by sperm from the prize bull. This is done in vitro, i.e. in a test tube.

7) The embryo is implanted into another cow, not the prize cow.

8) This surrogate cow mum carries the calf, and gives birth to it.

The main problem with selective breeding like this is that the same alleles keep appearing (and many others are lost). So a disease could wipe out an entire population if there are no resistant alleles. (See the Biology book for more info.)

Cloning is done by *Transplanting a Cell Nucleus*

Clones are genetically identical organisms.

1) The nucleus of an egg cell is removed — this leaves the egg cell without any genetic information.

2) Another nucleus is inserted in its place. This is a diploid nucleus from a cell of a different animal and is complete with all its genetic information.

See Biology Revision Guide for more information about cells, mitosis and zygotes.

3) The cell is stimulated so that it starts dividing by mitosis, as if it was a normal fertilised egg.

4) There are risks with cloning. Embryos formed by cloning from adult cells don't tend to develop normally.

5) The first mammal to be cloned from an adult cell was a sheep called "Dolly".

There are *Ethical Worries* about Cloning

1) If it's possible to clone mammals like Dolly the sheep, there's no reason why it shouldn't be possible to clone humans as well.

2) Many people don't want human cloning to ever happen. (An evil dictator might make an army of clones, and destroy the Galaxy, or something.)

3) Laws have been passed in several countries making research into the cloning of humans illegal.

4) Some people are in favour of cloning human body parts for use in transplant surgery. However, other people feel that this is morally wrong.

Learn this page — come on, get a mooooove on...

Selective breeding (where you take your best cows and breed from them) applies to crops too — it's the same basic principle, anyway. Cereals have been selectively bred from different grasses. But these selectively bred plants may need special conditions, like extra minerals, for example.

Gene Technology

Personally, if I found some T-Rex DNA I'd probably leave it where it was. But, science fiction apart, DNA is pretty interesting stuff. Which, as you'd expect, also means it's pretty complicated.

DNA carries the Genetic Code   *Also see the Biology book.*

The "twisted ladder" structure of DNA was eventually figured out in 1953, by Watson and Crick. They had spent months studying X-ray diffraction photographs obtained by Franklin and Wilkins.

DNA is a double-stranded helix (spiral) made up of nucleotides. Each nucleotide has a "base" — which can be any one of adenine (A), thymine (T), guanine (G) and cytosine (C). A on one strand always joins onto T on the other, and G on one strand always joins with C on the other. This is called base-pairing.

DNA carries the code to make proteins. Proteins are made of long chains of amino acids. Along a length of DNA, the order of bases determines which protein is made. Each set of three bases form a "code" for a particular amino acid. E.g. a triplet of TGG (in that order) would cause tryptophan to be added. TGG is called a "codon" for tryptophan, by the way.

DNA, RNA and Ribosomes Work Together to Make Protein

1) The two strands of DNA separate. RNA nucleotides join onto one of the strands, matching up by base-pairing. A strand of messenger RNA (mRNA) is formed. This process is called transcription.

Messenger RNA

2) mRNA travels from the cell nucleus out into the cytoplasm, until it reaches a ribosome.

Messenger RNA

Protein

Ribosome

3) The job of the ribosome is to stick amino acids together to make a polypeptide (protein), following the order of amino acids coded by the mRNA.

Messenger RNA

There are 'U's here instead of 'T's here because RNA has uracil instead of thymine.

Transfer RNA (tRNA), with three bases that match up with the mRNA code for an amino acid

Each tRNA carries a specific amino acid with it.

4) Inside the ribosome, the tRNA molecules match up with the mRNA strand by base-pairing, carrying their amino acid with them. As they join on, the amino acids bond together to form a protein chain.

Mistakes in Copying DNA to RNA cause Mutations

Examples: 1) inserting bases that shouldn't be there, e.g. ATTCG to ATTGCG, 2) not copying a base that should be there, e.g. ATTCG to ATTG, 3) copying a piece of DNA the wrong way around, 4) moving a sequence of bases to the wrong place, e.g. CGCCTATTCG to CATTCGGCCT

Ionising radiation makes mutations more likely. Mutagens are chemicals that cause mutation.

Not surprised we get mutations — who'd remember all that...

What a devil of a page to learn. First off, refresh yourself on what you already know about DNA. Then set about learning the big diagram in the middle. And make sure you know your tRNA from your mRNA.

Genetic Fingerprinting

DNA testing — it's amazing what they can do nowadays.
Anyway, impressed or not, you still have to learn this stuff.

Genetic Fingerprinting Pinpoints Individuals

1) Your DNA is unique — unless you have an identical twin, in which case you'll both have identical DNA.

2) DNA fingerprinting/genetic fingerprinting is a way of comparing DNA samples to see if they come from the same person or from two different people.

3) DNA fingerprinting is used in forensic science. DNA (from hair, skin flakes, blood, semen etc) taken from a crime scene is compared with a DNA sample taken from a suspect.

4) DNA testing can also be used in paternity tests — to check if a man and a child are father and son.

5) Some people would like there to be a national genetic database of everyone in the country. That way, DNA from a crime scene could be checked against everyone in the country to see whose it was. But there are ethical problems with treating everyone as a potential suspect in every crime. There are also scientific problems — false positives are too likely.

HOW IT WORKS

1) Special enzymes are used to cut DNA. They cut the DNA at every place where they recognise a particular section of code.

2) How often that bit of code comes up depends on where the cutting site comes up — if it comes up several times, it'll be cut into lots of little bits, and if it doesn't come up, it'll stay in one long length.

3) The DNA bits are treated using a process a bit like chromatography. (They're suspended in a gel, and an electric current is passed through the gel. The DNA tries to get to the negative electrode. Small bits travel faster than big bits, so they get further through the gel.)

4) The DNA is "tagged" with a radioactive marker. Then it's X-rayed. This shows up the bits of DNA. The pattern of lines on the DNA "blot" is the unique DNA fingerprint.

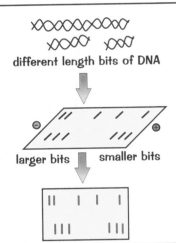

different length bits of DNA

larger bits   smaller bits

Radioactive Probes are used to Find Genes

Sometimes you might want to know if you have a particular gene (e.g. if you're at risk of an inherited disease like Huntington's chorea). This is how the tests are done.

1) A sample of DNA is isolated from white blood cells. It's cut into bits with enzymes, and each bit is spliced into a loop of bacterial DNA. The bacteria containing the sample are grown on agar jelly in a petri dish.

2) A fabric disc is used to blot up some of the bacteria from the dish. A test piece of DNA, "tagged" with a radioactive isotope, is added to the disc. The piece of DNA is complementary to the gene that you're looking for (i.e. it'll join onto it by base-pair matching).

Found 'em...

3) The tagged DNA attaches to the gene that you're looking for. You then look for this tagged DNA (or "gene probe") using UV light or radiation. Any glowing spots are where the probe has attached to DNA on the petri dish.

4) The bacteria containing the gene you're after are in the place in the dish corresponding to the glowing spot on the disc.

So the trick is — frame your twin and they'll never get you...

This is tricky to learn — I reckon writing a mini-essay on this stuff is a pretty good way to start. As you write your essay, jot down all the bits you're struggling with. Then you'll have a smaller list of things to learn. Once you've learnt them, do another mini-essay, etc. Hey — at least it's not Maths.

Agriculture and the Environment

And now for a page on how crop growth and the environment interact...

Crop growth is affected by the Environment

Soil pH affects how well plants grow

1) Enzymes in plants are affected by pH — certain plants will grow better in acidic conditions, while others prefer alkaline or neutral.

2) To test soil pH, you can add water to a small sample of soil and shake it. Then dip a strip of pH paper in the soil water — it changes colour depending on the pH.

3) Lime (calcium carbonate) can be added to soils that are too acidic to make them more alkaline. Humus (organic matter) can be added to soils that are too alkaline to make them more acidic.

soil and water — pH paper

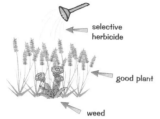

selective herbicide

good plant

weed

Weeds are unwanted plants

1) Weeds are a problem because they compete with crop plants. They have to be controlled using machines or chemicals.

2) Many chemical weedkillers (herbicides) are selective — they only kill the weeds and not the crops.

Crop growth can cause Long-Term Problems

1) Crop plants remove minerals from the soil. Expensive fertilisers then have to be added to replace the lost minerals.

2) Inorganic fertilisers like ammonium nitrate increase crop production. However, they can pollute rivers and other water courses. They also allow more intensive farming methods, which can lead to a breakdown of the soil structure.

3) When crops are grown for long periods in the same place, pests can increase in number. Insect damage leaves plants more vulnerable to disease. Pesticides may then have to be used to kill the pests.

4) A solution is that different crops can be grown in different fields and rotated each year. Crop rotation can lead to less mineral loss, less need for fertilisers, and can cut down on pests.

Farming methods can Improve Plant Quality

Controlled environments can create ideal conditions

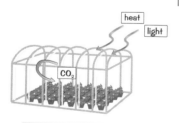

heat
light
CO₂

1) Hydroponics is where the plants are grown on a surface like gravel instead of soil. They are bathed with water and receive the right balance of dissolved minerals for healthy growth.

2) Greenhouses can help speed up photosynthesis. The warm, light atmosphere is perfect for photosynthesis. Extra carbon dioxide can even be added to speed things up even more.

See also the Biology book.

Plants can be genetically modified to improve food production

1) Crop plants can be made resistant to pests and herbicides to minimise potential damage, or allow you to use more herbicide.

2) Genetic engineering can also be used to increase nutritional quality and even extend shelf-life.

3) However, there are fears that genetically modified plants could damage ecosystems...

Get your head round this blooming lot...

This is pretty straightforward stuff — how the environment affects crop growth and how crop growth affects it back. But remember... there are moral and ethical issues in genetic engineering, and you have to weigh the possible drawbacks against the potential benefits. It's all good 21st century fun.

Revision Summary for Section Two

So you think you've learnt these Biotechnology pages, eh... Well, there's only one way to really find out. And you know what that is, I'll bet. It's obvious... I mean, there's a whole load of questions staring you in the face — chances are, it's got to involve those in some way. And sure enough, it does. Just write down the answers to all these questions. Then go back over the section and see if you got any wrong. If you did, then you need a bit more revision, so go back and have another read of the section and then have another go. It's the best way to make sure you actually know your stuff.

1) What is a "culture medium"?
2) What nutrients does agar jelly usually contain?
3) What is a petri dish?
4) Why is it important to sterilise 'micro-organism growing equipment' before use?
5) What is used to transfer micro-organisms to the culture medium? How is it sterilised?
6) At what temperature are bacterial cultures usually incubated in the class lab?
   Is this hotter or colder than in industrial labs?
7) Give two advantages of using micro-organisms for food production.
8) What micro-organisms are used in the manufacture of blue cheese?
9) Explain what is meant by "malting".
10) Name one liquid yeast is used to make.
11) What is added to beer to give it its bitter flavour?
12) Name three types of micro-organism involved in the production of soy sauce.
13) Why must soy sauce be pasteurised before bottling?
14) What is a fermenter?
15) Give four examples of conditions that are controlled inside an industrial fermenter.
16) Give two examples of products made inside a fermenter.
17) Describe how biotechnology could help developing countries feed themselves.
18) What micro-organism is used to make penicillin?
19) What does yeast ferment to make ethanol?
20) What can ethanol be used for in some countries (apart from the obvious)?
21) What are the two main components of biogas?
22) How does a batch digester differ from a continuous digester?
23) What is biogas used for?
24) What waste products are used to make biogas?
25) In artificial insemination, how is semen extracted from suitable bulls, and how is it stored?
26) Where does fertilisation of the cow's egg occur?
27) Does the genetic mother of the calf actually give birth to the calf?
28) Briefly describe the process of cloning a mammal by transplant of a cell nucleus.
29) Is the nucleus that's implanted into the egg cell haploid or diploid?
30) Give examples of ethical concerns about cloning.
31) What are the four bases in DNA?
32) How many bases make up the code for one amino acid?
33) What is the name of the process by which messenger RNA is formed?
34) What is the role of ribosomes in making protein?
35) What is the role of transfer RNA in making protein?
36) What's the term for when a mistake is made in copying DNA to RNA?
37) Why is DNA fingerprinting so useful in forensic science? How does it work?
38) Why do you end up with different length pieces of DNA?
39) How are the different length bits sorted out?
40) What are the ethical problems involved in keeping a genetic database of the whole population?
41) Describe how to test the pH of a sample of soil. How could you make it more acidic/alkaline?
42) Describe how crop growth can cause long term problems.
43) Describe two methods that can be used to improve the quality of crops.

Systems Of Classification

It seems to be a basic human urge to want to classify things — that's the case in biology, anyway. There are millions of species, so having a way to group and name them is pretty important.

Classification Systems can be Natural or Artificial

1) Natural classification systems put organisms into groups based on genetic similarities. For example, bats, whales and humans have a similar bone pattern in their forelimbs, and are all genetically related. A natural system of classification would reflect these similarities.

2) An artificial system of classification places organisms into groups based on similarities which are not due to genes. For example, a shark and a porpoise both live in the sea, and might be grouped together, although they're not very similar at all — one's a fish and one's a mammal.

3) Biologists use natural methods of classification to group living organisms.

4) Living things are divided into kingdoms (e.g. the animal kingdom, the plant kingdom). Kingdoms are then subdivided into smaller and smaller groups. An example of one of these smaller groups is a genus.

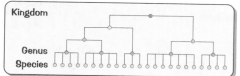

5) A genus is a group of closely related species — and a species is a group of closely-related organisms that breed to produce fertile offspring.

The Binomial System gives everything a Two-part Name

1) John Ray was the first person to use a sensible natural system of classification — he divided organisms according to structural features rather than things like colour.

2) Carl Linnaeus then mixed some of Ray's ideas with some of his own. It was Linnaeus who came up with the binomial system for naming species.

3) It's called the binomial system because each organism is given a two-part Latin name. The first part of the name refers to the genus that the organism belongs to and the second part refers to the species.

> **Example:**
> Humans are known as Homo sapiens. 'Homo' is the genus that they belong to and 'sapiens' is the species.

Species Diversity is Pretty Important for a Habitat

1) Species diversity is thought to be pretty important nowadays. Species diversity is a measure of:
   i) the number of different species there are in a particular habitat,
   ii) how many organisms of each species there are in that habitat.

2) The higher the species diversity for a habitat, the less likely it is that species living there will die out.

3) One reason for this is that food webs in habitats with a high species diversity are more complex, and so if a food source disappears, there are more likely to be alternatives available.

4) It's important to conserve species for cultural, aesthetic, economic (and moral) reasons:

> **Cultural** Removing certain species from an environment could disrupt traditional ways of life (e.g. certain plants in Africa contain dyes used for tribal markings).

> **Aesthetic** Bird sanctuaries and national parks are enjoyed by loads of people — losing species diversity would be a bit of a blow.

> **Economic** Many organisms can be sold for food, medical purposes, fibres for clothing, etc.

Binomial system — uh, oh, sounds like maths...

Biodiversity is a word that gets bandied about quite a lot these days. It's a bit like species diversity, but only deals with the number of species in a particular habitat, whereas species diversity measures the number of each species present as well. But anyway, they're pretty important, so learn them.

Animals and their Breathing

Amphibians live on land but their breeding habits and method of gas exchange mean they're dependent upon water to a certain extent, i.e. they have to keep returning to water for a quick dip. Reptiles on the other hand have features that make them better adapted to living on land.

Amphibians Breathe partly through their Skin

1) Adult amphibians have simple lungs, but their skin also plays an important part in their breathing process.

2) Oxygen moves into the animal and carbon dioxide moves out through the skin, as well as via the lungs. To help with this, an adult amphibian's skin has to be kept moist (the skin produces mucus to help with this).

3) However, this means the skin can't be waterproof. This lack of waterproofing means the amphibian would lose too much water if it lived in a dry environment. The same applies to amphibians' eggs — they're not waterproof and would dry out on land (forcing amphibians to lay their eggs in water).

4) Amphibians' bumpy skin makes the surface area for gas exchange bigger.

5) Tadpoles have a different system of breathing. They live in water and have gills for gas exchange.

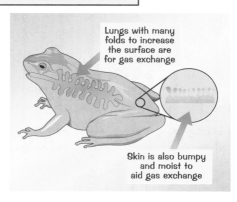

Lungs with many folds to increase the surface are for gas exchange

Skin is also bumpy and moist to aid gas exchange

Unshelled eggs are laid in water. Eggs hatch into tadpoles.

Reptiles are better adapted for Life on Land

1) Reptiles have scaly, waterproof skin, which stops them losing too much water on land.

2) Reptile eggs also have a waterproof shell — this means they won't dry out and so reptiles don't have to lay eggs in water.

3) Gas exchange takes place only through lungs on land.

Fish use their Gills to Breathe

1) Fish can only breathe when they're in water.

2) A constant supply of oxygen-rich water flows through the open mouth of the fish, and is then forced through the gill slits near the side of the head.

3) Water helps support the gills — it keeps the gill folds separated from each other.

4) Gas exchange occurs at the gills (which are highly folded to increase the surface area). The gills have a good blood supply, which takes oxygen away from the gills and brings carbon dioxide towards them.

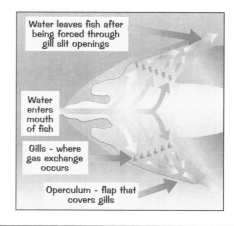

Water leaves fish after being forced through gill slit openings

Water enters mouth of fish

Gills - where gas exchange occurs

Operculum - flap that covers gills

Memory like a goldfish — not if you revise...

'Gas exchange' gets lots of mentions on this page — it sounds really fancy and complicated, but all it really means is that business of getting oxygen into your bloodstream and carbon dioxide out. Remember — this is biology you're doing now... simple things usually have complicated names.

Vertebrates

Vertebrates — now they're creatures with a bit of <u>backbone</u>.

Vertebrates *have a* Backbone *and an* Internal Skeleton

1) Fish, amphibians, reptiles, birds and mammals are all <u>vertebrates</u>, meaning they all have a <u>backbone</u> and an <u>internal skeleton</u>.

2) The job of the <u>skeleton</u> is to <u>support</u> the body and allow it to <u>move</u>, as well as to <u>protect</u> vital <u>organs</u>.

3) <u>Bones</u> contain <u>living cells</u>. These cells lay down <u>salts</u> containing <u>calcium</u> and <u>phosphate</u> (which make the bones <u>hard</u>, and so more difficult to compress, bend or stretch) and produce <u>proteins</u> (which stop the bones from being <u>brittle</u>).

4) Parts of some bones have a <u>spongy structure</u> which helps them to withstand stresses from <u>various directions</u>.

5) Some large bones also have a <u>space</u> inside. This space contains <u>bone marrow</u>, which is where new <u>blood cells</u> are made.

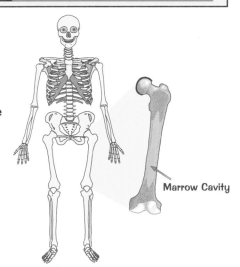

Marrow Cavity

Joints *allow the* Bones *to* Move

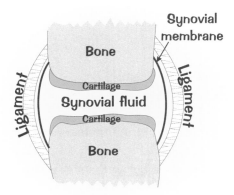

Synovial membrane

Bone

Ligament

Cartilage

Synovial fluid

Cartilage

Ligament

Bone

1) The bones at a joint are held together by <u>ligaments</u>. Ligaments have <u>tensile strength</u> (i.e. you can pull them and they don't snap easily) but are pretty <u>elastic</u> (stretchy).

2) The ends of bones are covered with <u>cartilage</u> to stop the bones <u>rubbing</u> together. And as cartilage can be slightly compressed, it can act as a <u>shock absorber</u>.

3) <u>Membranes</u> at joints release oily <u>synovial fluid</u> to <u>lubricate</u> the joints, allowing it to move more easily.

Muscles Pull *on Bones to* Move *them*

1) Bones are attached to muscles by <u>tendons</u>.

2) Like ligaments, tendons have <u>tensile strength</u>. However tendons are <u>not</u> very stretchy.

3) Muscles move the bones at a joint by <u>contracting</u> (becoming <u>shorter</u>). This means that muscles can only <u>pull</u> on bones to move a joint — they <u>can't</u> push.

4) This is why muscles usually come in <u>pairs</u> (called <u>antagonistic pairs</u>). When one muscle in the pair contracts, the joint moves in one direction — and when the other contracts, the joint moves in the <u>opposite</u> direction.

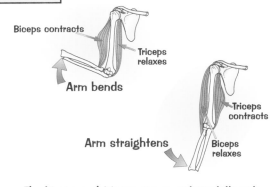

Biceps contracts

Triceps relaxes

Arm bends

Triceps contracts

Arm straightens

Biceps relaxes

The <u>biceps</u> and <u>triceps</u> are an antagonistic pair of muscles — they bend and straighten the <u>arm</u>.

I'm not a vertebrate — I'm completely spineless...

You need to know <u>all</u> the functions of the skeleton — but learning them should be pretty easy, I reckon. Then you're on to the trickier task of sorting out your <u>tendons</u> from your <u>ligaments</u>, and your <u>cartilage</u> from your <u>synovial fluid</u>. Cover the page, write it all down, and see what you got wrong.

Fish and Birds

Something on this page is a bit <u>fishy</u>... but that's because half the page is about <u>fish</u>. Aha-ha-ha-ha-ha.

Fish are quite good at Swimming

As you might expect, fish are pretty competent <u>swimmers</u>. But then again they should be, as they've got various <u>adaptations</u> which makes them suited to an <u>aquatic</u> life. It's all down to <u>evolution</u>.

1) A fish's <u>streamlined</u> body reduces <u>friction</u>.
2) Most fish have a <u>swim bladder</u>. This is a <u>gas-filled</u> sac in the body, which aids <u>buoyancy</u>.
3) Fish have their muscles arranged in a <u>zig-zag</u> pattern — this helps to produce <u>wave-like</u> contractions to move the fish through the water.

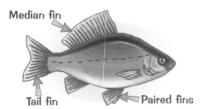
Median fin
Tail fin
Paired fins

4) The <u>tail fin</u> has a large <u>surface area</u> helping to push water <u>backwards</u> (and the fish forwards).
5) <u>Median fins</u> increase the vertical <u>surface area</u> of the fish, and so help keep the fish <u>upright</u>.
6) <u>Paired fins</u> on the body allow the fish to <u>steer</u>, <u>brake</u>, and make swift <u>direction changes</u>.

Birds are well-adapted for Flying

Most birds are expert flyers. Well they would be — their bodies are <u>evolved</u> to allow them to generate <u>loads of lift</u>, but at the same time remain pretty <u>lightweight</u>.

1) A bird's <u>streamlined</u> body-shape reduces <u>air resistance</u>.
2) Birds' <u>bones</u> have a <u>honeycombed</u> structure, making them <u>strong</u> but <u>light</u>.
3) A bird's large <u>sternum</u> (breastbone) gives a large <u>surface area</u> and a rigid frame to attach the powerful <u>flight muscles</u> to.
4) <u>Flight feathers</u> are <u>strong</u> yet <u>hollow</u> (again, making them <u>lighter</u>). And the feathers have interlocking <u>barbs</u>, creating a flat, streamlined surface.
5) When <u>gliding</u>, the shape of the wings helps to create higher pressure <u>below</u> them than <u>above</u> them, creating <u>lift</u>.
6) When <u>flapping</u>, the wings' large <u>surface area</u> makes them very effective at pushing <u>downwards</u> (and so lifting the bird up). In fact, a bird's feathers are arranged so that when the bird moves its wings <u>downwards</u> there are <u>no gaps</u> between the feathers, helping to <u>propel</u> the bird. But when the bird moves the wings <u>upwards</u>, <u>gaps</u> between the feathers let air through, stopping downward <u>drag</u>.

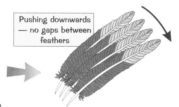
Pushing downwards — no gaps between feathers

Moving upwards — gaps between feathers

The Pentadactyl Limb is a very Common Structure

1) A <u>pentadactyl limb</u> is one with <u>five digits</u> (e.g. humans have five <u>fingers</u> at the end of each arm).
2) The <u>wings</u> of a bat and a bird have a similar structure to a human arm, except birds have <u>fewer digits</u> (finger-like projections) and fewer <u>wrist bones</u> — these were lost as a result of <u>evolution</u>.

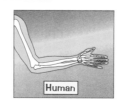
Human

Bat

I love being a bird — you just can't beak it...

<u>Pentadactyl limbs</u> are very common throughout the animal kingdom. Amphibians, reptiles, birds and mammals all have variations on the pentadactyl limb theme, which I for one think is pretty amazing. The same goes for the way birds have become so ideally suited for <u>flying</u>. They're incredibly <u>well-engineered</u>.

Invertebrates Feeding

The eating habits of invertebrates — that's what they want you to know about. What could be lovelier...

Mussels _Filter_ Plankton _from Water_

Mussels live in water where they filter feed on microscopic organisms called plankton. This involves:

1) pulling water (and plankton) through the body using the beating action of tiny hairs called cilia.
2) sieve-like gills trapping the plankton (but not the water).
3) the captured food being transported from the gills to the mouth using the action of another set of cilia.

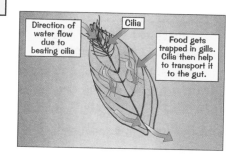

Direction of water flow due to beating cilia — Cilia — Food gets trapped in gills. Cilia then help to transport it to the gut.

Mosquitoes _are specially adapted for_ Sucking Blood

1) A mosquito's mouthparts include a sharp tube called a proboscis, which can penetrate skin.
2) Muscles in the mosquito's throat help it to draw blood into the proboscis from capillaries near their victim's skin.
3) Their saliva contains a substance that stops the blood from clotting. Worse than that — a mosquito's saliva may also contain parasites which can cause malaria.

Parasites live on or in other species called the host. The parasite gains food but causes harm to the host.

4) The malarial parasite is a single-celled organism that enters red blood cells, where it feeds and reproduces. The red blood cells then burst open, causing an awful fever. (See pages 2-3 for more info.)

Aphids, butterflies and houseflies also use tubes to eat

1) Aphids use a tube called a stylet to pierce a plant's phloem and steal the sugary fluid.
2) Butterflies use a long proboscis to slurp nectar from flowers.
3) Houseflies use their proboscis to drop saliva onto solid food. The saliva dissolves the food and allows the fly to then vacuum it up using its proboscis.

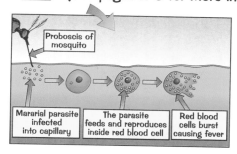

Proboscis of mosquito

Mararial parasite infected into capillary — The parasite feeds and reproduces inside red blood cell — Red blood cells burst causing fever

Metamorphosis — _a_ Larva _changes to its_ Adult Form

1) During metamorphosis, the make-up of an animal's body changes completely — this happens when the animal becomes an adult (like, for example, when a tadpole turns into a frog — or when a caterpillar becomes a butterfly).
2) The young form of the creature is a larva, but later the larva undergoes metamorphosis and turns into the adult form. (So, for example, a frog's larva is a tadpole.)
3) The advantage of this is that the creature can make use of different foods and habitats at different stages of its life.

i) A blowfly undergoes metamorphosis.
ii) A blowfly egg hatches into a larva called a maggot, which lives and feeds on rotting meat.
iii) The larva then turns into a pupa — this is where all the dramatic changes take place (metamorphosis).
iv) Eventually the adult blowfly emerges from the pupa.

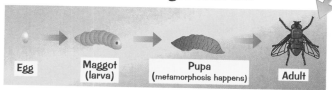

Egg — Maggot (larva) — Pupa (metamorphosis happens) — Adult

Aphids, butterflies and houseflies — they're all suckers...

Some charming topics there to put you off your dinner. But it all goes to show how well-adapted creatures become to their environment. If we humans were to become equally well-suited to our typical environment, we'd all have enormous bottoms so that we wouldn't need chairs, and ball-point fingers.

Teeth

Fairly unsurprisingly, mammals' <u>teeth</u> are well adapted to the type of <u>food</u> they eat.

Different Teeth perform Different Functions

1) <u>Mammals</u> use teeth to <u>obtain</u> food, and to <u>break</u> it up into small pieces before <u>digestion</u>.

2) So although front and back teeth have the same basic <u>structure</u> (with a <u>root</u> embedded in the gum and an enamel-covered <u>crown</u>) they differ quite a bit in <u>shape</u> and <u>size</u>.

The <u>arrangement</u> of different types of teeth in a mammal's jaw is called its <u>dentition</u>.

There are four types of <u>tooth</u>, and they have different <u>shapes</u> depending on the <u>function</u> they perform.

① <u>Incisors</u> — these have <u>sharp edges</u> for <u>cutting</u> into food (and in the case of carnivores for pulling flesh off bones).

② <u>Canines</u> — these are <u>long</u> and <u>pointed</u> (like <u>fangs</u>) for <u>tearing</u> at food (and for <u>catching</u> it, if you're a carnivore).

③ & ④ <u>Pre-molars and molars</u> — these are <u>wide</u> and <u>flat</u> with ridges for <u>crushing</u> and <u>grinding</u> food.

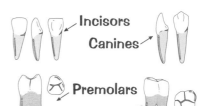

Incisors
Canines
Premolars
Molars

Humans' teeth need to deal with All Sorts

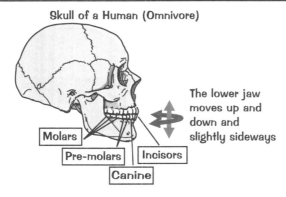

Skull of a Human (Omnivore)

The lower jaw moves up and down and slightly sideways

Molars
Pre-molars
Incisors
Canine

1) <u>Humans</u> are <u>omnivorous</u> (we eat both <u>meat</u> and <u>vegetable</u> matter), and so our teeth have to be able to deal with <u>various</u> kinds of food.

2) This means that human teeth are <u>not</u> highly <u>specialised</u> like those of animals that eat mainly <u>one kind</u> of food. For example, human incisors and canines are less well developed than those of <u>carnivorous</u> mammals like dogs.

3) Human teeth are used mainly for <u>cutting</u> and <u>crushing</u> various foods — and to a lesser extent <u>grinding</u> it.

Dogs' teeth are adapted for a mainly Carnivorous Diet

<u>Dogs</u> have teeth and jaws adapted for a <u>carnivorous</u> diet (containing only <u>meat</u>).

Dogs do eat some vegetable matter. They're not completely carnivorous.

1) Dogs have six small <u>incisor</u> teeth for <u>stripping</u> meat off bones.

2) Behind them are four prominent curved <u>canine</u> teeth, which can <u>hold</u> and <u>kill</u> prey.

3) The <u>premolars</u> and <u>molars</u> of the lower jaw bite <u>inside</u> those of the upper jaw, resulting in a <u>shearing</u> action (like scissors), which is good for <u>cutting</u> flesh. This <u>scissor action</u> is made even more effective by the fact that a dog's jaw moves only <u>up and down</u> (and not side-to-side).

4) The <u>carnassial</u> teeth (types of <u>molar</u>) are particularly large and important for <u>shearing</u> and <u>crushing</u> bones.

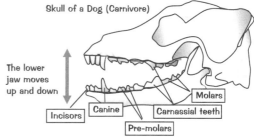

Skull of a Dog (Carnivore)

The lower jaw moves up and down

Incisors
Canine
Pre-molars
Carnassial teeth
Molars

Go on — get your teeth into this little lot...

Blah blah blah adapted blah blah blah environment blah blah blah evolution blah blah blah...
Hmmm, yeah, I reckon you might be getting the picture by now, eh. Things <u>adapt</u> to their environment, because if they don't, they don't get to hang around for long. So they would, wouldn't they.

Digestive Systems

Different diets need different kinds of digestive system. This is why the structure of various mammals' guts varies so much. So now I've got you 'interested', on with the show...

Mammals use Bacteria to help Digest Cellulose

1) The walls of plant cells are made of cellulose.

2) However, mammals don't produce an enzyme to break down cellulose.

3) That means that herbivores (animals that eat only plants) need some way of breaking down the cellulose.

4) That means making use of cellulose-digesting bacteria. Plant eaters have these bacteria somewhere in their gut — they break down the cellulose into sugars which the animal can easily digest.

Ruminants Chew the Cud

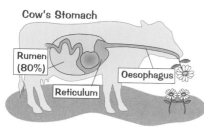

Cow's Stomach

Rumen (80%)

Oesophagus

Reticulum

1) Animals that chew cud, like sheep and cattle, have an enlarged 'stomach' that's divided into four different chambers.

2) Food is first swallowed and passed into the first chamber, where it's formed into balls of cud (partially digested food).

3) It's then returned to the mouth and chewed again. Lovely.

4) The next time the food's swallowed, it passes into a second chamber called the rumen, which makes up 80% of the total stomach volume.

5) It's in the rumen that the food gets mixed with huge amounts of saliva and cellulose-digesting bacteria. The rumen's basically a big fermenting chamber, and releases loads of carbon dioxide and methane.

Rabbits eat their own Whoopsies

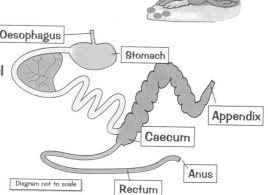

Mmmm... Poo.

Oesophagus

Stomach

Appendix

Caecum

Anus

Diagram not to scale

Rectum

1) Rabbits deal with cellulose in a different way.

2) They have an enlarged caecum and appendix which contain the cellulose-digesting bacteria.

3) This part of the gut is situated between the small and large intestine. Unfortunately, this means that the cellulose-digesting bacteria don't actually reach the food until after most of the nutrients have been absorbed.

4) So food that's gone through the rabbit's gut once is turned into soft faecal pellets, which are then eaten again immediately. (This behaviour is known as coprophagy.)

5) When the pellets go through the stomach a second time, the cellulose has been broken down by the bacteria, meaning that the rest of the food can be digested.

Carnivores don't need Cellulose-digesting Bacteria

Carnivores (e.g. cats) have no need for cellulose digesting bacteria (as they don't eat plants). As a result, their digestive systems don't have special sections for them.

Coprophagy — don't try it at home...

The relationship between cellulose-digesting bacteria and herbivores is an example of mutualism, as both organisms benefit — herbivores obtain sugars from the cellulose, and the bacteria get cellulose and other nutrients. Everyone's a winner. And they said a page about animals eating their own poo would be dull.

Exercise

All animals (including humans) are incredibly well adapted to their environment. But things as complex as humans need a bit of looking after, which is where regular exercise can really help. Even so, you need to be careful not to overdo things. As my nan (probably) says, "Everything in moderation." Wise words, indeed.

Exercise Increases the Heart Rate

1) Muscles are made of muscle cells. These use oxygen to convert glucose to energy (this process is called respiration), which is used to contract the muscles.

2) An increase in muscle activity requires glucose and oxygen to be supplied at a faster rate to the muscles, and removal of extra carbon dioxide and heat from the muscles.

3) This is why physical activity increases your breathing rate and the speed at which the heart pumps — to supply muscles with more oxygen and remove extra CO_2. The pulse will also remain higher than normal for a while after the exercise has finished.

4) How high the pulse goes, and how long it remains high depends on:
   i) the fitness of the person (a less fit person will have a smaller heart that has to work harder and will take longer to return to normal).
   ii) the extent and demands of the exercise.

Run, Sam, run. Here comes the bull...

Many people enjoy the challenge of exercise too.

Exercise is Good for You...

Gradually increasing the work that muscles, bones and joints do develops strength and fitness.

Regular exercise can:
   i) maintain muscle tone, so that the fibres are tensed and ready to contract,
   ii) increase muscle strength — regular use of muscles means they increase in size and are more able to do work,
   iii) keep joints working well,
   iv) maintain a good supply of blood to heart, lungs and muscles.

...but Overdoing things can lead to Injury

Putting too much strain on your muscles, bones and joints can lead to sprains, strains and other nasties.

(1) **Strains** — where muscles are overstretched and damaged.

(2) **Sprains** — where ligaments are damaged after being extended beyond their normal range of movement.

(3) **Dislocations** — where bones are forced out of the joint. This is most common at the hip and shoulder.

Too much keep-fit makes your head spin round — like in the Exercist...

A fairly basic page this one — nothing too taxing here really. But just because it's not too taxing doesn't mean you can be blasé about it — it still needs to be learnt properly. Cover the page, write down what you remember, then check to see what you got wrong. And do it again if you need to.

Revision Summary for Section Three

And so, the end is near, and now you face the final curtain... yep, the revision summary. Thirty-six questions full of nothing but joy and excitement, just waiting to be answered. Having a go at these questions is the best way to find out if you've really learned Section Three or if it has gone in one ear and out the other. (Or should that be "in one eye and out the other" — dunno.) So write down your answers, and then have a look to see how many you got wrong. And if you didn't get 36 out of 36, go back and have another look at the section... and then try the questions again. More fun than cutting your toenails.

1) Explain the difference between natural and artificial systems of classification.
2) Which system do biologists use?
3) What is a species?
4) In the binomial system each organism is given a two part name. What does each part refer to?
5) What two things does species diversity measure?
6) Why is it good for habitats to have a high species diversity?
7) Give three reasons for conserving species.
8) What two things do adult amphibians use to breathe?
9) Why can't amphibians live in dry environments?
10) Why can reptiles lay their eggs on land but amphibians can't?
11) Where does gas exchange happen in fish?
12) What do all vertebrates have in common?
13) Where are new blood cells made?
14) What holds bones together at joints?
15) What is the fluid which lubricates the joints called?
16) How do muscles move the bones at a joint?
17) Describe four adaptations fish have for underwater life.
18) What makes birds' bones strong but light?
19) What is a pentadactyl limb?
20) Describe how mussels feed on plankton from water.
21) What disease do mosquitoes sometimes carry?
22) What is it called when a larva changes into its adult form? Give an example of this.
23) Name four types of tooth and say what each is used for.
24) What does omnivorous mean?
25) Describe four ways dogs' teeth are adapted for a carnivorous diet.
26) What are the walls of plant cells made of?
27) How do cows break down cellulose so that they can digest it?
28) What happens to food in the first chamber of sheep's stomachs?
29) What is the name of the second chamber in sheep's stomachs? What happens to food there?
30) What two things contain cellulose digesting bacteria in rabbits?
31) Why do rabbits eat the soft faecal pellets they produce?
32) Why don't carnivores have special sections for cellulose digesting bacteria in their digestive systems?
33) What do muscle cells use to convert glucose to energy? What is this process called?
34) What effect does exercise have on your breathing and heart rate?
35) Describe two ways in which exercise is good for your muscles.
36) What is the difference between strains and sprains?

Acids and Bases

Acids and bases — there's loads been written about these before. But as that rather splendid comedian of the early 1980s, Jimmy Cricket, used to say, "There's more." Sigh... those were the days.

Acids are all about Hydrated Protons

1) When mixed with water, all acids release hydrogen ions — H⁺ (an H⁺ ion is just a proton).

E.g.
$$HCl(g) + water \longrightarrow H^+(aq) + Cl^-(aq)$$
$$H_2SO_4(l) + water \longrightarrow 2H^+(aq) + SO_4^{2-}(aq)$$

But HCl doesn't release hydrogen ions until it meets water — so hydrogen chloride gas isn't an acid.

2) The positive H⁺ ion attracts the slightly negative side of a water molecule. (Water is 'polar' — the oxygen-side of the molecule is slightly negative, while the hydrogen-side is slightly positive.)

3) This proton with bits of water in tow is now written 'H⁺(aq)' and given the fancy name of 'hydrated proton'. And it's these hydrated protons that make acids acidic, if you like.

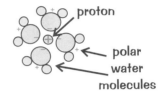
proton
polar water molecules

Bases want to Grab H⁺ ions

1) Not all bases dissolve in water, but those that do are called alkalis.

2) Alkalis form OH⁻ ions (hydroxide ions) when in water.

E.g. $$Ammonia: NH_3(g) + H_2O \longrightarrow NH_4^+(aq) + OH^-(aq)$$

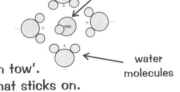
hydroxide
water molecules

3) Hydroxide ions are also hydrated, i.e. they also have water molecules 'in tow'. But because they're negatively charged, it's the positive side of water that sticks on.

4) A bloke called Arrhenius reckoned that this was what made bases special — the fact that they released OH⁻ ions. (But since not all bases are soluble, this couldn't be the whole story.)

5) However, Lowry and Brønsted made things a bit more general. They came up with definitions that work for both soluble and insoluble bases:

Acids put H⁺(aq) ions into a solution — i.e. they're proton donors.

Bases remove H⁺(aq) ions from a solution — i.e. they're proton acceptors.

Acids can be Strong or Weak

1) Strong acids (e.g. sulphuric, hydrochloric and nitric) ionise completely in water. This means that every hydrogen atom is released to become a hydrated proton (so there are loads of H⁺(aq) ions).

2) Weak acids (e.g. ethanoic, citric) ionise only very slightly, i.e. only some of the hydrogen atoms in the compound are released (maybe less than 1%) — so only small numbers of H⁺(aq) ions are formed.

Strong acid: $HCl + water \longrightarrow H^+ + Cl^-$ Weak acid: $H_2CO_3 + water \rightleftharpoons H^+ + HCO_3^-$

Note the 'reversible reaction' symbol for a weak acid.

3) The pH of an acid or alkali is a measure of the concentration of H⁺(aq) ions in a solution. Strong acids have a pH of about 0 or 1, while the pH of a weak acid might be 4, 5 or 6.

4) The pH of an acid or alkali can be measured with a pH meter or with Universal Indicator paper (or by seeing how fast a sample reacts with, say, magnesium). See page 37 for more methods.

5) There are strong and weak alkalis too. The hydroxides of sodium and potassium, KOH and NaOH, are strong (pH 14), while ammonia is a weak alkali (pH 9-10).

Save the bases — become a proton donor...

You need to know the difference between acids that are 'dilute/concentrated', and acids that are 'weak/strong'. 'Weak' and 'strong' describe the proportion of hydrogen atoms released, whereas 'dilute' and 'concentrated' just describe how 'watered down' your acid is. So you can have a dilute but strong acid.

Solubility of Salts

Something is <u>soluble</u> if it <u>dissolves</u> — like <u>sugar</u> when you put it in tea (hurrah).
Something is <u>insoluble</u> if it <u>doesn't dissolve</u> — like <u>sand</u> when you put it in tea (boo, hiss).

Solubility — Learn the Proper Definitions

The <u>solubility</u> of a substance in a given solvent is the number of <u>grams of the solute</u> (the solid) that dissolve in <u>100 g of the solvent</u> (the liquid) at a particular <u>temperature</u>.

E.g. at <u>room temperature</u>, about 35 g of sodium chloride (NaCl) will dissolve in 100 g of water.

A <u>saturated solution</u> is one that cannot hold any more solid <u>at that temperature</u> — and you have to be able to see <u>solid</u> on the bottom to be certain that it's saturated.

Solubility Rules — Learn them, Okay

1) As a general rule, most ionic compounds are soluble in water, while most covalent compounds are not.

2) Unfortunately, there are quite a few rules that you need to know off by heart.

A SALT IS USUALLY SOLUBLE IN WATER IF...

① IT'S A SALT OF SODIUM, POTASSIUM OR AMMONIUM

② IT'S A NITRATE (NO_3^-), CHLORIDE (Cl^-) OR A COMMON ETHANOATE (CH_3COO^-)
Exceptions: silver chloride, AgCl and lead chloride, $PbCl_2$

③ IT'S A SULPHATE SO_4^{2-} — but barium sulphate and lead sulphate are insoluble, and calcium sulphate is only a little soluble.

A SALT IS USUALLY INSOLUBLE IN WATER IF...

④ IT'S A CARBONATE, (CO_3^{2-}) — except those of sodium, potassium and ammonium.

⑤ IT'S A HYDROXIDE, (OH^-) — except those of sodium, potassium and ammonium.

Solubility Curves show when a solution is Saturated

1) A <u>solubility curve</u> plots the <u>mass of solute</u> dissolved in a saturated solution at <u>various temperatures</u>.

2) The solubility of most solids <u>increases</u> as the temperature <u>increases</u>.

3) This means that <u>cooling</u> a saturated solution will usually cause some solid to <u>precipitate out</u>.

4) The <u>mass</u> of solute <u>precipitated</u> (or the mass of <u>crystals</u> formed) by <u>cooling</u> a solution can be calculated from a solubility curve:

Draw lines perpendicular to both axes through the temperatures in the question, then subtract the smaller mass from the larger — that difference must precipitate out on cooling.

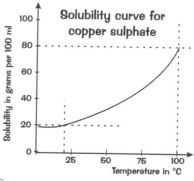

<u>Example</u>: How much copper sulphate will precipitate out when 100 ml of a saturated solution is cooled from 100 °C to 20 °C? <u>Answer</u>: 80 g – 20 g = <u>60 g</u>

My brain is saturated — I feel facts pouring out of my ears...

Those five solubility rules (plus the exceptions) are worth learning properly. So cover the page and write down the <u>three</u> types of substance that are <u>soluble</u>, together with the <u>exceptions</u>. Then do the same for the <u>two insoluble</u> substances. And if you got anything wrong, try again. And again if necessary.

Making Salts

Salts have a <u>positive</u> bit and a <u>negative</u> bit, e.g. sodium chloride (Na^+Cl^-), lead nitrate ($Pb^{2+}(NO_3^-)_2$), and so on. There are <u>four</u> main methods for making salts which you need to know about:

1) Reaction between the Elements

1) This works well when you want to combine a <u>fairly reactive metal</u> with a <u>non-metal gas</u>, e.g. reacting aluminium foil or iron wool with chlorine.

2) You just pass a reactive gas over a <u>heated</u> metal in a combustion tube. This method's good because you end up with a <u>pure</u>, <u>dry</u> <u>salt</u>.

E.g. $2Fe + 3Cl_2 \longrightarrow 2FeCl_3$

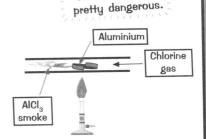
This is easy, but pretty dangerous.

Aluminium
Chlorine gas
$AlCl_3$ smoke

2) Making Insoluble Salts — Precipitation Reactions

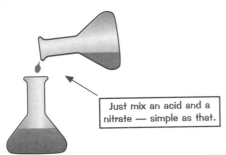
Just mix an acid and a nitrate — simple as that.

1) If the salt you want to make is <u>insoluble</u>, you can use a <u>precipitation reaction</u>.

2) You just need to pick the right <u>acid</u> and <u>nitrate</u>, then mix them together. E.g. if you want to make <u>lead chloride</u> (which is insoluble), mix <u>hydrochloric acid</u> and <u>lead nitrate</u>.

3) Once the salt has precipitated out (and is lying at the bottom of your flask), all you have to do is <u>filter</u> it from the solution, <u>wash</u> it and then <u>dry</u> it on filter paper.

E.g. $Pb(NO_3)_2(aq) + 2HCl(aq) \longrightarrow PbCl_2(s) + 2HNO_3(aq)$

3) Making Soluble Salts — but NOT of Na, K or NH₄

1) You need to pick the right <u>acid</u>, plus a <u>metal carbonate</u> or <u>metal hydroxide</u> (as long as it's <u>insoluble</u>).

2) You add the <u>carbonate</u> or <u>hydroxide</u> to the <u>acid</u> until <u>all</u> the acid is neutralised. (The excess carbonate or hydroxide will just <u>sink</u> to the bottom of the flask when all the acid has reacted.)

3) Then <u>filter</u> out the excess carbonate, and <u>evaporate</u> off the water — and you should be left with a <u>pure</u>, <u>dry</u> salt.

You can't use Na, K or NH_4 carbonates or hydroxides, as they're soluble (so you can't tell whether the reaction has finished).

<u>Filtering</u> — to get rid of the excess carbonate or hydroxide.

E.g. you can use <u>copper carbonate</u> and <u>nitric acid</u> to make <u>copper nitrate</u>, or <u>iron hydroxide</u> and <u>hydrochloric acid</u> to make <u>iron chloride</u>.

$CuCO_3(s) + 2HNO_3 \longrightarrow Cu(NO_3)_2(aq) + CO_2 + 2H_2O$
$Fe(OH)_2(s) + 2HCl \longrightarrow FeCl_2(aq) + 2H_2O$

And if the metal is between calcium and copper in the reactivity series, you can just use the metal itself instead of a carbonate or hydroxide.

4) Making Salts of Na, K or NH₄

1) <u>Sodium</u>, <u>potassium</u> and <u>ammonium</u> salts are made by neutralising an <u>acid</u> with a <u>hydroxide</u>.

2) So to make <u>sodium chloride</u>, react <u>hydrochloric acid</u> with <u>sodium hydroxide</u> (and then <u>evaporate</u> off the water).

E.g. $NaOH(aq) + HCl(aq) \longrightarrow NaCl(aq) + H_2O$

Be worth your salt — learn how to make them...

That first method's obvious, but the rest have lots of details, unfortunately. One thing the other methods have in common is that you have to use an acid. Then remember <u>IN</u> — <u>I</u>nsoluble salts are made with <u>N</u>itrates, and <u>SHoCk</u> — <u>S</u>oluble salts are made with <u>H</u>ydroxides and <u>C</u>arbonates.

Gases: Solubility and Collection

Gases — making them and testing for them. This is where the book gets interesting again. But not very.

All Gases are Soluble — to some extent, anyway

1) 'Chlorine water' is a solution of chlorine gas in water (unsurprisingly). It's used as bleach for the paper and textile industries, and also to sterilise water supplies (as bleaching bacteria kills them).

2) The amount of gas that dissolves depends on the pressure of the gas above it — the higher the pressure, the more gas that dissolves. (Fizzy drinks initially contain a lot of dissolved carbon dioxide. But when you take the cap off, the pressure's released and a lot of CO_2 fizzes out of solution.)

3) Gases become less soluble as the temperature of the solvent increases, which is exactly the opposite of solids. (Aquatic life needs dissolved oxygen, but pollution and warm water discharged from towns and industry raises the temperature and lowers the dissolved oxygen levels, causing problems.)

The Collection Method depends on the Gas

A side-arm flask is the standard apparatus to use when you're trying to collect gases. But what you connect the side arm to depends on what it is you're trying to collect...

(1) Gas Syringe

You can use a gas syringe to collect pretty much any gas.

(2) Collection over Water

1) You can use a delivery tube to bubble the gas into an upside-down measuring cylinder or gas jar filled with water.

2) But this method's no good for collecting things like hydrogen chloride or ammonia (because they just dissolve in the water).

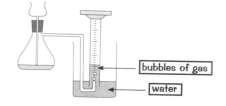

bubbles of gas

water

(3) Upward / Downward Delivery

Use upward delivery to collect 'lighter than air' gases (e.g. H_2).
Use downward delivery to collect 'heavier than air' gases (e.g. CO_2).

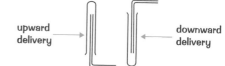

upward delivery

downward delivery

Learn the Tests for these Common Gases

1) Hydrogen — burns with a squeaky pop when ignited.
(This is an explosive gas, so be careful when you use it.)

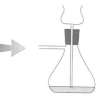

Squeaky pop!!

2) Hydrogen chloride — turns damp blue litmus red.
(Don't breathe this in — it won't do you any good.)

3) Ammonia — turns damp red litmus blue.
(This has a very strong smell.)

glowing splint

4) Oxygen — relights a glowing splint.

5) Sulphur dioxide — damp orange dichromate paper goes green.
(This also has a very strong smell.)

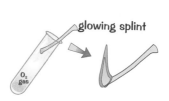

CO_2 gas

6) Carbon dioxide — turns limewater milky.

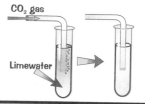

Limewater

Making gas — now don't pretend you never have...

On a practical note — when you're collecting a gas, it's a good idea to allow the reaction to run a little before connecting the actual collecting gubbins. This 'flushes' air through the apparatus, meaning the gas you collect will be pure(ish). This is an easy page — so take my advice and enjoy it while it lasts.

Tests for Positive Ions

Say you've got a compound, but you <u>don't know</u> what it is.
Well, you'd want to <u>identify</u> it... that's only natural. And that's what the next two pages are about.

Flame Tests — Spot the Colour

Compounds of some metals burn with a characteristic colour, as you
see every November 5th. So, remember, remember...

(i) <u>Sodium</u>, Na^+, burns with an orange flame.
(ii) <u>Potassium</u>, K^+, burns with a lilac flame.
(iii) <u>Calcium</u>, Ca^{2+}, burns with a brick-red flame.
(iv) <u>Copper</u>, Cu^{2+} burns with a blue-green flame.

(See also Instrumental
Methods on page 37.)

Add NaOH and look for a Coloured Precipitate

1) Many <u>metal hydroxides</u> are <u>insoluble</u> and precipitate out of solution when formed.

2) Some of these hydroxides have a <u>characteristic colour</u>.

3) The idea behind this test is to add a few drops of <u>sodium hydroxide</u> solution to 'test solutions' of your mystery compound. Hopefully, you'll form one of these <u>insoluble hydroxides</u>.

4) If you do, the colour tells you which <u>hydroxide</u> you've got, and so what the '<u>metal bit</u>' of your mystery compound must be...

"Metal"	Colour of precipitate	Ionic Reaction
Calcium, Ca^{2+}	White	$Ca^{2+}(aq) + 2OH^-(aq) \rightarrow Ca(OH)_2(s)$
Copper(II), Cu^{2+}	Blue	$Cu^{2+}(aq) + 2OH^-(aq) \rightarrow Cu(OH)_2(s)$
Iron(II), Fe^{2+}	Sludgy green	$Fe^{2+}(aq) + 2OH^-(aq) \rightarrow Fe(OH)_2(s)$
Iron(III), Fe^{3+}	Reddish brown	$Fe^{3+}(aq) + 3OH^-(aq) \rightarrow Fe(OH)_3(s)$
Aluminium, Al^{3+}	White at first. But then redissolves in excess NaOH to form a colourless solution.	$Al^{3+}(aq) + 3OH^-(aq) \rightarrow Al(OH)_3(s)$ then $Al(OH)_3(s) + OH^- \rightarrow Al(OH)_4^-(aq)$
Ammonium, NH_4^+	No precipitate, but the smell of ammonia (see also litmus test on next page)	

Ionic Equations show just the Useful Bits of Reactions

The reactions in the above table are <u>ionic equations</u>. Ionic equations are 'half' a full equation, if you like. They just show the bit of the equation you're <u>interested</u> in — nothing else.

Example: $Ca^{2+}(aq) + 2OH^-(aq) \longrightarrow Ca(OH)_2(s)$

1) This shows the formation of (solid) <u>calcium hydroxide</u> from the <u>calcium ions</u> and the <u>hydroxide ions</u> in solution. And it's the formation of this that helps identify the compound.

2) The <u>full</u> equation in the above reaction would be (if you started off with <u>calcium chloride</u>, say):
$CaCl_2(aq) + 2NaOH(aq) \longrightarrow Ca(OH)_2(s) + 2NaCl(aq)$

3) But the formation of <u>sodium chloride</u> is of no great interest here — it's not helping to <u>identify</u> the compound, after all.

4) So the ionic equation just concentrates on the <u>good bits</u>.

Chemistry joke*: "Are you a cation?" "Yes, I'm positive"

An easy page, kind of. The principles are easy enough, but it's learning all those darn <u>colours</u> that's a pain in the neck. You could try some kind of <u>word association</u> thing, e.g. in the sodium hydroxide test, <u>copper</u> gives a <u>blue</u> precipitate — so remember that a copper is a policeman, and policemen wear blue.

Tests for Negative Ions

And it's not just positive ions you can test for, you'll be pleased to know.
Yep, you can also test for negative ions, and so the fun goes on...

The Acid Test — use Hydrochloric Acid

The gases given off by salts reacting with HCl can be used for identification.

Carbonates (CO₃) give off CO₂

With dilute acids, carbonates (CO_3^{2-}) give off CO_2 (which you can test for with limewater — see page 32).

$$2H^+(aq) + CO_3^{2-}(s) \longrightarrow CO_2(g) + H_2O(l)$$

Sulphites (SO₃) give off SO₂

Sulphites, (SO_3^{2-}), give off SO_2 when mixed with dilute hydrochloric acid.
You can test for this with damp dichromate paper (see page 32).

$$SO_3^{2-}(s) + 2H^+(aq) \longrightarrow SO_2(g) + H_2O(l)$$

Test for Sulphates (SO₄) and Halides (Cl, Br, I)

You can test for certain ions by seeing if a precipitate is formed after these reactions...

Sulphate ions, SO₄²⁻

To test for a sulphate ion (SO_4^{2-}), add dilute HCl, followed by barium chloride, $BaCl_2$.
A white precipitate of barium sulphate means the original compound was a sulphate.

$$Ba^{2+}(aq) + SO_4^{2-}(aq) \longrightarrow BaSO_4(s)$$

Chloride, Bromide or Iodide ions, Cl⁻, Br⁻, I⁻

To test for chloride, bromide or iodide ions, add dilute nitric acid (HNO_3), followed by silver nitrate ($AgNO_3$).
A chloride gives a white precipitate of silver chloride.
A bromide gives a cream precipitate of silver bromide.
An iodide gives a yellow precipitate of silver iodide.

$$Ag^+(aq) + Cl^-(aq) \longrightarrow AgCl(s)$$

The other reactions are the same as this, except the chloride ion is replaced with bromide or iodide.

Use Litmus Indicator to check for Acidity and Alkalinity

Testing for $H^+(aq)$ and $OH^-(aq)$ ions can be done using red or blue litmus indicator.
Blue litmus turns red if $H^+(aq)$ ions are present, i.e. if the solution is an acid.
Red litmus turns blue if $OH^-(aq)$ ions are present, i.e. if the solution is an alkali.

And if you add an ammonium salt to a hydroxide, ammonia's formed, which is easy to test for — see p32.

The Test for Nitrates (NO₃) is a bit Dangerous

If none of the above tests tell you what the negative ion is, then test to see if it's a nitrate...

1) Mix some of the compound with a little aluminium powder.
2) Then add a few drops of sodium hydroxide solution and heat.

This test is a bit dangerous, so ask before you do it.

Any nitrate is reduced to ammonia, which can be tested for with litmus (see above).

$$NO_3^- \longrightarrow NH_3$$ The NaOH/Al mix is a good reducing agent and reduces NO_3^- ions to NH_3.

Don't be so negative about Science — Maths is much harder...

Four tests — testing for nine different things. Again, it's all the details that are the trickiest things to remember, but you've just got to know them. Learn the details for one test, then cover the page and write everything down. If you get anything wrong, do it all again. You need to do this for all the tests.

Quantitative Chemistry

Run for your lives now, while you've still got the chance — it's <u>equations</u> and stuff.

Avogadro's Law — One Mole of Gas Occupies 24 dm³

<u>Learn</u> this fact — you're going to <u>need</u> it:

> One mole of <u>any gas</u> always occupies <u>24 dm³</u> (= 24 000 cm³) at standard temperature and pressure (STP — 25°C and 1 atmosphere)

dm³ is just a fancy way of writing 'litre', so 1 dm³ = 1000 cm³

Example 1: What's the volume of 4.5 moles of chlorine at STP?

Answer: 1 mole = 24 dm³, so 4.5 moles = 4.5 × 24 dm³ = <u>108 dm³</u>

Example 2: How many moles are there in 8280 cm³ of hydrogen gas at STP?

Answer: Number of moles = $\dfrac{\text{Volume of gas}}{\text{Volume of 1 mole}}$ = $\dfrac{8.28}{24}$ = <u>0.345 moles</u>

Don't forget to convert from cm³ to dm³.

Triangle: Volume over (Moles × 24)

Concentration = No. of Moles ÷ Volume

The <u>concentration</u> of a solution is measured in <u>moles per dm³</u> (i.e. <u>moles per litre</u>).
So 1 mole of stuff dissolved in 1 dm³ of solvent has a concentration of <u>1 mole per dm³</u>.

> Concentration = $\dfrac{\text{Number of Moles}}{\text{Volume}}$

Triangle: M over (C × V)

Example 1: What's the concentration of a solution with 2 moles of salt in 500 cm³?

Answer: Easy — you've got the number of moles and the volume, so just stick it in the formula...

Concentration = $\dfrac{2}{0.5}$ = <u>4 moles per dm³</u>   Convert the volume to litres (i.e. dm³) first by dividing by 1000.

Example 2: How many moles of sodium chloride are in 250 cm³ of a 3 molar solution of sodium chloride?

Answer: Well, 3 molar just means it's got 3 moles per dm³. So using the formula... *3 molar is sometimes written '3 M'.*

Number of moles = concentration × volume = 3 × 0.25 = <u>0.75 moles</u>

Crystals sometimes trap Water of Crystallisation

1) Magnesium sulphate crystals have a formula of $MgSO_4.6H_2O$ — this means that as the salt <u>crystallises</u>, six water molecules are trapped for each particle of magnesium sulphate.

2) This water <u>evaporates</u> when the crystals are <u>heated</u>, so your crystals weigh less. Cue the question...

Example: 25 g of $CuSO_4.xH_2O$ gave 16 g of $CuSO_4$ after heating. Find x.

You have to work out how many molecules of water are trapped for each copper sulphate particle. So...

1: *Write the equation:* $CuSO_4.xH_2O(s) \longrightarrow CuSO_4(s) + xH_2O(g)$

2: *Put in the masses:*   25 g $\longrightarrow$ 16   9

You're told the first two, so the mass that's lost must be due to the water.

3: *Convert to moles:*   16 g of $CuSO_4$ is 16 / 160 = 0.1 moles.
   9 g of H_2O is 9 / 18 = 0.5 moles.

> For this you need the equation:
> No. of moles = Mass (in grams) ÷ M_r
> (where M_r is the molecular mass).
> It's in the Chemistry book.

4: *Work out the ratios:*
   0.1 moles of $CuSO_4$ combine with 0.5 moles of H_2O.
   So 1 mole of $CuSO_4$ combines with 5 moles of H_2O.
   So x must be 5 — and the formula is $CuSO_4.5H_2O$.

Concentration — makes revision so much easier...

This looks worse than it is — really it's a couple of formula triangles and a 4-step method (shocker).

Titration

Titrations are used to find out the concentration of acid or alkali solutions. They're also handy when you're making salts of soluble bases.

Titrations need to be done Accurately

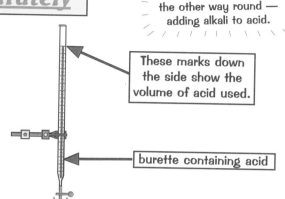

You can also do titrations the other way round — adding alkali to acid.

1) Titrations allow you to find out exactly how much acid is needed to neutralise a quantity of alkali.

2) You put some alkali in a flask, along with some indicator, e.g. phenolphthalein.

3) Add the acid, a bit at a time, to the alkali using a burette — giving the flask a regular swirl. Go especially slowly when you think the alkali's almost neutralised.

4) The indicator changes colour when all the alkali has been neutralised, e.g. phenolphthalein is pink in alkalis, but colourless in acids.

5) Record the amount of acid used to neutralise the alkali. It's best to repeat this process a few times, making sure you get the same answer each time.

These marks down the side show the volume of acid used.

burette containing acid

alkali and indicator

The Calculation — Work out the Numbers of Moles

Now for the calculations... basically, you're trying to find the number of moles of each substance. A formula triangle is pretty handy here, I reckon. (And it's the same one as on page 35.)

Example: Suppose you start off with 25 cm³ of sodium hydroxide in your flask, and you know that its concentration is 0.1 moles per dm³.

You then find from your titration that it takes 30 cm³ of sulphuric acid (of an unknown concentration) to neutralise the sodium hydroxide.

Find the concentration of the acid.

Step 1: Work out how many moles of the 'known' substance you have:

Number of moles = concentration × volume = 0.1 × (25 / 1000) = 0.0025 moles

Step 2: Write down the equation of the reaction...

$$2NaOH + H_2SO_4 \longrightarrow Na_2SO_4 + 2H_2O$$

...and work out how many moles of the 'unknown' stuff you must have had.

Using the equation, you can see that for every two moles of sodium hydroxide you had... ...there was just one mole of sulphuric acid.

So if you had 0.0025 moles of sodium hydroxide... ...you must have had 0.0025 ÷ 2 = 0.00125 moles of sulphuric acid.

Step 3: Work out the concentration of the 'unknown' stuff.

Concentration = number of moles ÷ volume
= 0.00125 ÷ (30 / 1000) = 0.0417 moles per dm³

Phenolphthalein in a flask — nothing complicated about that...

The method above is the same as writing one formula triangle for the acid and one for the alkali, filling in the corners you're given, and then finding all the others. It works every time. One thing that you do have to be careful about with these, though, is that you're using the right units for the volume.

Instrumental Methods

Machines can be used to follow a neutralisation reaction, or more generally to analyse a substance.

You can Monitor Reactions using Machines

The neutralisation point of a reaction (i.e. when an alkali or acid is just neutralised) is usually found by using an indicator (e.g. universal indicator) in a titration, but there are other methods...

① Use a pH Meter

This is probably the best way to monitor the pH change during a titration. You stick a probe in the solution and you get a reading on an attached machine of what the pH is.

② Measure the Heat Change

Since a neutralisation reaction is exothermic (i.e. it gives out heat), you can measure the temperature and detect when no more heat is given off.
Even better, after the reaction's finished, excess acid will start to cool the solution.

③ Use a Conductivity Meter

1) A conductivity meter measures the conductivity of a solution (i.e. how well it conducts electricity).

2) Conductivity depends on the number of ions in solution — more ions means greater conductivity.

3) The number of ions decreases during a titration as OH^- ions are converted to H_2O by the acid's H^+ ions. After the end point, the conductivity increases again as more H^+ ions are added.

Machines can also Analyse Unknown Substances

1) Machines can also be used to analyse samples of chemicals. They're more accurate, quicker, and can detect even the tiniest amounts of substances.

2) They're useful for medical purposes, police forensic work, environmental analysis, checking whether an athlete has taken a banned substance, analysis of products in industry and so on.

3) Rapid advances in electronics and computing have made more advanced analysis easily possible.

① Atomic Emission Spectroscopy

1) This is essentially a flame test machine, and is used for identifying elements.

2) A tiny sample is injected into a very hot flame, and the whole spectrum of light is analysed. Each element present in the sample produces a unique spectrum.

3) It's much faster and much more reliable than can be done with the human eye.

beep beep... vrrrr... definitely sodium

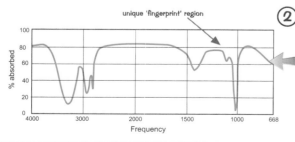

unique 'fingerprint' region

② Infra-red Spectroscopy

1) Most carbon compounds absorb infra-red light.

2) The compound under investigation is placed in the path of infra-red radiation and the amount of each frequency that's absorbed is plotted. The pattern of absorbance is unique for every compound. This 'fingerprint' allows identification of individual compounds.

But they still haven't invented revision machines...

This is the kind of chemistry I can get my head round — bung something in a machine and wait for it to do its stuff. Anyway... for those spectroscopy things, make sure you remember that 'atomic emission' identifies atoms (i.e. elements), while 'infra-red' is for identifying compounds. What could be simpler...

Revision Summary for Section Four

Now then... let's see how you've got on with that little lot. It's not the nastiest section in the world, but then again, it's not the nicest either. There's an awful lot of detail, but on the plus side, that means there's loads of marks to pick up on it. Unfortunately, there's no way of getting round the fact that you've got to know stuff like definitions, solubilities, and how to make stuff. So practise on these little beauties, and if you get any wrong, try them again. And keep trying until you can do them all without so much as breaking wind... or sweat even.

1) What do acids form in water?
2) How did Lowry and Brønsted define an acid?
3) How did Lowry and Brønsted define a base?
4) What makes an acid 'strong'?
5) How can you be certain that a solution is saturated?
6) Is a salt of sodium or potassium likely to be soluble or insoluble?
7) If a salt is a hydroxide, is it likely to be soluble or insoluble?
8) A saturated solution contains 50 g of solute at 60 °C and 30 g at 40 °C.
   What mass precipitates out in cooling the saturated solution from 60 °C to 40 °C?
9) Describe how you could make an insoluble salt.
10) Describe how you could make a soluble copper salt.
11) Describe how you could make a sodium salt.
12) Name four different methods of collecting a gas.
13) Gases are often made in a side-arm flask fitted with a thistle funnel.
    Why must the tube from the funnel go below the liquid level?
14) Which gases must never be collected over water? Why?
15) How would you test for the gases H_2, O_2, CO_2, NH_3, HCl and SO_2?
    Describe each test, including how you would recognise a positive result.
16) What are the flame test colours of K^+, Na^+, Ca^{2+}, Cu^{2+}?
17) Describe the characteristics of the precipitates of Al^{3+}, Ca^{2+}, Cu^{2+}, Fe^{2+} and Fe^{3+} with NaOH(aq).
18) Write ionic equations for the reactions in the question above.
19) How can an ammonium salt be identified?
20) What are the tests for CO_3^{2-} and SO_3^{2-}? What is the name of the SO_3^{2-} ion?
21) How do you test for a suspected chloride or sulphate?
22) How do you test for a nitrate?
23) What is the formula mass M_r of $CaCO_3$ (Ca = 40, C = 12, O = 16)?
24) How many moles are there in 687.5 g $CaCO_3$?
25) A salt G has a formula mass of 68. It has a hydrated salt $G.xH_2O$. On heating 7 g of the hydrated salt, 3.6 g were lost. Find x.
26) What is the purpose of titration?
27) 25 cm^3 of sodium hydroxide solution, 0.15 mol dm^{-3}, was neutralised by 22.5 cm^3 nitric acid, HNO_3.
    What is the concentration of the nitric acid?
28) An indicator can be used to identify the neutralisation point of a reaction.
    Describe three other methods.
29) State three advantages of using machines for analysing stuff.
30) Name two machines that can identify unknown substances.

Water

Water, water, everywhere... but then again, that's probably what you'd expect on this page, given the title.

The Sea is Sodium Chloride and Other Salts in Solution

Salt — tonnes of it, in fact.

1) Sea water (also known as brine) is a solution of many different salts — mainly sodium chloride.
2) Salt is extracted from the sea by evaporation.
3) Shallow lagoons (or "salt pans") are flooded with sea water. The Sun evaporates the water and leaves the salt behind.

Dissolved Carbon Dioxide Makes Water Slightly Acidic

1) Carbon dioxide is quite soluble in water.
2) It dissolves to form carbonic acid (H_2CO_3), a weak acid (see page 29 for more info), and so water tends to be slightly acidic.

$$CO_2 + H_2O \rightarrow H_2CO_3$$
$$H_2CO_3 \rightarrow H^+(aq) + HCO_3^-(aq)$$

Tap Water Must be Purified

Fresh water contains nasties, which need to be removed before it's supplied to our houses:

> i) micro-organisms,
> ii) clay particles (a colloid, see page 40),
> iii) chemicals causing bad taste/bad smell,
> iv) too much acidity.

1) The micro-organisms are removed by adding chlorine — this kills the bacteria.
2) Tiny colloidal particles are removed from the water by adding aluminium sulphate. The positive aluminium ions (Al^{3+}) bond onto negatively charged clay particles, causing them to precipitate out.
3) The water is then left to settle, and filtered.
4) Nasty tastes and odours are removed by passing the water through "activated carbon" filters, or with "carbon slurry".

A slurry is a suspension of solid particles in a liquid — so it's a type of colloid.

5) Excess chlorine is removed with sulphur dioxide.

$$SO_2 + 2H_2O + Cl_2 \rightarrow 4H^+ + SO_4^{2-} + 2Cl^-$$

6) A limestone slurry is used to make sure the water isn't too acidic.

$$2H^+ + CaCO_3 \rightarrow Ca^{2+} + CO_2 + H_2O$$

Loads of Cl^-, Ca^{2+} and SO_4^{2-} ions are in the water anyway from where it's seeped through the ground. These 'extra' ones make little difference.

Iron(III) Hydroxide in Water Causes Problems

Old iron pipes sometimes allow iron(III) hydroxide into drinking water. This causes a few problems.

1) Vegetables turn brown when cooking.
2) Tea takes on an inky colour and a bitter taste.
3) Rusty stains are left on clothes after washing.

Water fantastic page this is...

Here's a fairly straightforward page. Not much to learn about sea water except how salt is extracted. You need to learn all the stages of purifying tap water. Learn all the stages, cover the page and then write them down. Then check to see if you missed any out. And if you did, do it all over again.

Colloids

Slurry is a kind of colloid. But the word 'colloid' sounds somehow more scientific than 'slurry'.

Colloids are Mixtures of Tiny Particles Dispersed in a Liquid

1) A colloid consists of really tiny particles of one kind of stuff dispersed in (i.e. mixed in with) another kind of stuff.

2) The particles can be bits of solid, droplets of liquid or bubbles of gas.

3) The particles are called the dispersed phase. It can be one substance, or it can be a mixture of substances.

4) The liquid that contains the particles is called the continuous phase. Again, it can be one substance, or it can be a mixture of substances.

5) Colloids don't separate out because the particles are so small, and they're often electrically charged (see below).

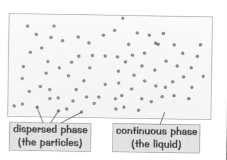

dispersed phase (the particles)   continuous phase (the liquid)

Three Kinds of Colloid — Sols, Emulsions and Foams

1) A sol is made from solid particles dispersed in liquid, e.g. clay particles in water, which don't settle out when the mixture is left to stand.

2) An emulsion is made from droplets of one liquid dispersed in another, e.g. emulsion paint or mayonnaise.

3) A foam is made of very small gas bubbles dispersed in a liquid, e.g. shaving foam.

Particles in a Colloid are Sometimes Charged

1) Charged particles attract water molecules to them.

2) Water molecules are polar — they have a slightly negative end, and a slightly positive end.

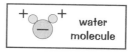

water molecule

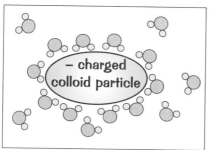

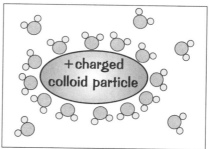

3) A coating of water molecules forms, keeping the particles dispersed in the water.

4) Charged colloid particles in a water-based continuous phase will stay dispersed, and won't clump together.

5) However, metal ions can cause particles of a colloid to clump together. They do this by attaching to the charged colloid particle and neutralising the charge on it.

6) When the colloid particle is no longer charged, it no longer has a protective coating of water molecules. So there's nothing to stop it sticking to other colloid particles.

Learning emulsions — better than watching paint dry...

There's nothing particularly difficult about the idea of a colloid. It's just tiny particles all spread out in a liquid. The only slightly tricky thing here is being able to explain why the particles don't all clump together, and how water molecules help keep them apart. It's all down to charge.

Hard Water

The water in your part of the country might be <u>hard</u> or it might be <u>soft</u>.
Hardness comes from <u>limestone</u>, <u>chalk</u> and <u>gypsum</u>.

Hard Water Makes Scum and Scale

1) <u>Hard water</u> won't easily form a <u>lather</u> with soap. It makes a <u>nasty scum</u> instead.

2) Hard water also forms <u>scale</u> (calcium carbonate) on the insides of pipes, boilers and kettles.
   <u>Scale</u> is a bit of a <u>thermal insulator</u>. This means that a <u>kettle</u> with <u>scale on the heating
   element</u> takes <u>longer to boil</u> than a <u>clean</u> non-scaled-up kettle. Scale can even <u>eventually
   block pipes</u>. Badly scaled-up pipes and boilers need to be <u>replaced</u> — at a cost.

3) Hard water also causes a <u>horrible scum</u> to form on the <u>surface of tea</u>.

4) <u>Non-soap detergents aren't affected</u> by hard water.

Hardness is Caused by Ca^{2+} and Mg^{2+} ions

These calcium and magnesium ions come from the salts <u>calcium sulphate</u>,
<u>magnesium sulphate</u>, <u>calcium carbonate</u> and <u>magnesium carbonate</u>.

1) <u>Calcium sulphate</u> and <u>magnesium sulphate</u> dissolve (just a little bit) in water.

2) <u>Calcium carbonate</u> and <u>magnesium carbonate</u> don't dissolve in water, but they will react with <u>acids</u>.

3) And since <u>CO_2</u> from the air <u>dissolves in rainwater</u> (forming <u>carbonic acid</u>, $CO_2 + H_2O \rightarrow H_2CO_3$),
   rainwater is slightly <u>acidic</u>.

4) This means that calcium carbonate and magnesium carbonate can react with rainwater to form
   <u>calcium hydrogencarbonate</u> ($H_2CO_3 + CaCO_3 \rightarrow Ca(HCO_3)_2$), which is <u>soluble</u>.

Hard Water Isn't All Bad

1) Ca^{2+} ions are good for healthy <u>teeth</u> and <u>bones</u>. They also slightly reduce the risk of <u>heart</u> disease.

2) Scale inside pipes forms a <u>protective coating</u>. It stops <u>metal ions</u>, e.g. <u>Pb^{2+}</u> and <u>Cu^{2+}</u>
   (from lead and copper pipes) getting into <u>drinking water</u>. It also protects iron pipes from <u>rust</u>.

Some Hardness Can be Removed

Hardness caused by dissolved <u>calcium hydrogencarbonate</u> or <u>magnesium hydrogencarbonate</u> is <u>temporary
hardness</u>. Hardness caused by dissolved <u>calcium sulphate</u> or <u>magnesium sulphate</u> is <u>permanent hardness</u>.

1) <u>Temporary hardness</u> is removed by <u>boiling</u>, e.g. calcium hydrogencarbonate <u>decomposes</u> to form
   insoluble $CaCO_3$. This <u>won't work</u> for permanent hardness, though. Heating a <u>sulphate</u> ion does <u>nowt</u>.
   (This calcium carbonate precipitate is the 'scale' on your kettle.)

$$Ca(HCO_3)_2 \rightarrow CaCO_3(s) + H_2O + CO_2$$

2) <u>Both types of hardness</u> are removed by adding <u>sodium carbonate</u>.
   The carbonate ions join onto the calcium or magnesium ions and make an <u>insoluble precipitate</u>.

e.g. $$Ca^{2+}(aq) + CO_3^{2-}(aq) \rightarrow CaCO_3(s)$$

3) <u>Both types of hardness</u> can also be removed by '<u>ion exchange columns</u>'. These clever bits of chemistry
   have lots of <u>sodium ions</u> (or <u>hydrogen ions</u>) and 'exchange' them for calcium or magnesium ions.

e.g. $$Na_2Resin(s) + Ca^{2+}(aq) \rightarrow CaResin(s) + 2Na^+(aq)$$ ('*Resin*' is a huge insoluble resin molecule.)

4) <u>Scale</u> is just <u>calcium carbonate</u>, and can be dissolved by <u>acid</u>. Which is nice to know.

Hard water — what, like ice...

Hard water's <u>annoying stuff</u>, to be sure. All that nasty scum and scale — yuck. It's slightly annoying to
learn about too — I'll grant you that. To make sure you <u>really know it all</u>, take care to learn all the
equations properly. You should be able to write them all down, with the <u>book closed</u>. Go on then...

Electrochemistry and Electrolysis

Molten Salts Conduct Electricity

A salt will conduct an electric current when molten. The salt is always broken up into elements.

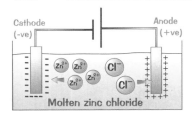

Cathode (-ve)   Anode (+ve)

Molten zinc chloride

You can melt zinc chloride using a Bunsen burner.

Electrons turn positive metal cations to atoms at the cathode (the –ve electrode):
E.g. $Zn^{2+}(l) + 2e^- \rightarrow Zn(l)$

Negative anions are oxidised (i.e. they lose electrons) to atoms at the anode (the +ve electrode): $2Cl^- \rightarrow Cl_2 + 2e^-$

Faradays and Coulombs are Amounts of Electricity

1) One amp flowing for one second means a charge of one coulomb has moved.

2) Generally, the amount of charge (Q, measured in coulombs) flowing through a circuit is equal to the current (I) multiplied by the time in seconds (t): $Q = It$

3) 96 000 coulombs (amps × seconds) is one faraday.

4) One faraday contains one mole of electrons.

1 A for 1 s = 1 C
$Q = I \times t$ (seconds)
96 000 C = 1 faraday
1 faraday = 1 mole of electrons

One Mole of Product needs 'n' Moles of Electrons

A sodium ion needs one electron to make a sodium atom. So one mole of sodium ions is gonna need one mole of electrons (one faraday) to make one mole of sodium atoms. But an ion with a 2^+ charge needs two moles of electrons to make one mole of atoms, and, guess what, three for a 3^+ charge...

$Na^+ + e^- \rightarrow Na$	1 mole of sodium ions	+ 1 mole of electrons	$\rightarrow$ 1 mole of sodium atoms
$Zn^{2+} + 2e^- \rightarrow Zn$	1 mole of zinc ions	+ 2 moles of electrons	$\rightarrow$ 1 mole of zinc atoms
$Al^{3+} + 3e^- \rightarrow Al$	1 mole of aluminium ions	+ 3 moles of electrons	$\rightarrow$ 1 mole of aluminium atoms

Use these Steps in Example Calculations

Example: If 5 amps flows for 20 minutes during the electrolysis of aqueous lead(II) chloride at STP, find (a) the mass of lead and (b) the volume of chlorine liberated. (PbCl2

1) Write out the TWO BALANCED HALF-EQUATIONS for each electrode.

$$Pb^{2+} + 2e^- \rightarrow Pb \text{ and } 2Cl^- \rightarrow Cl_2 + 2e^-$$

Writing the half-equations is easier if you remember that the full equation is: $PbCl_2 \rightarrow Pb + Cl_2$

2) Calculate the NUMBER OF FARADAYS.

First calculate amps × seconds = 5 × 20 × 60 = 6000 coulombs.

Number of faradays = 6000 / 96 000 = 0.0625 F

3) Calculate the NUMBER OF MOLES OF PRODUCT

(divide the number of faradays by the number of electrons in the half-equation).

0.0625 ÷ 2 = 0.03125 moles for each.

4) WRITE IN THE M_r VALUES from the Periodic Table to work out mass of solid products.

Mass of lead = 207 × 0.03125 = 6.5 g

5) Use the "ONE MOLE OF ANY GAS TAKES UP 24 DM^3" rule to find the volume of gas products.

To find the volume of bromine, multiply the number of moles by 24 dm^3.

Volume = 0.03125 × 24 = 0.75 dm^3

Faster shopping at Tesco — use Electrolleys...

Electrolysis is covered in the Chemistry revision guide if you need to check. What you need to learn here is how to work out the amount of product when you're given the amount of electricity.

Electrochemical Cells

You can use different metals and a salt solution to actually make electricity. It's how batteries work.

An *Electrochemical Cell* Makes *Electricity*

A simple electrochemical cell is made of two different metals dipped into a salt solution and connected by a wire (not in the solution).

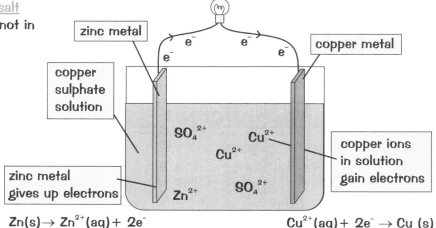

1) Atoms of the more reactive metal (zinc, in this case) get rid of electrons and turn into positive ions.

2) The electrons flow through the wire to the less reactive metal (copper).

3) Dissolved metal ions take up electrons, and turn into metal atoms, which get deposited onto the electrode made of the less reactive metal. In this case, copper ions from the copper sulphate solution get deposited onto the copper cathode.

$$Zn(s) \rightarrow Zn^{2+}(aq) + 2e^-$$

$$Cu^{2+}(aq) + 2e^- \rightarrow Cu(s)$$

4) Remember those electrons passing through the wire — that's electric current. Electric current passing through the bulb makes the bulb light up.

5) The electrode which releases electrons is the positive electrode — the anode. The electrode which takes electrons is the negative electrode — the cathode.

Electrons flow from the positive to the negative.

6) This is really a kind of displacement reaction. Zinc is more reactive than copper, so it displaces copper in the solution.

Half-Equations — *What Happens at the Electrodes*

This is the half-equation for what happens at the anode. This is LOSS OF ELECTRONS — OXIDATION:

$$Zn_{(s)} \rightarrow Zn^{2+}_{(aq)} + 2e^-$$

This is the half-equation for what happens at the cathode. This is GAIN OF ELECTRONS — REDUCTION:

$$Cu^{2+}_{(aq)} + 2e^- \rightarrow Cu_{(s)}$$

Add them together and you get the full ionic equation:

$$Zn_{(s)} + Cu^{2+}_{(aq)} \rightarrow Zn^{2+}_{(aq)} + Cu_{(s)}$$

Remember "OIL RIG" Oxidation Is Loss (of electrons) Reduction Is Gain (of electrons)

Remember:

OXIDATION IS LOSS OF ELECTRONS — REDUCTION IS GAIN

Everything that happens in an electrochemical cell is down to loss of electrons on one side, and gain of electrons on the other side. That's what pushes the electrons through the circuit. And electrons moving through a circuit means... ELECTRIC CURRENT.

Reduction is gain — and they say Chemistry isn't confusing...

All this business of making electricity with ions and cathodes and anodes can seem a bit weird. The way to deal with it is to learn carefully what happens at the anode, and what happens at the cathode. It doesn't matter at all that it seems weird. All you have to do is learn, bit by bit, what's going on.

Electrochemical Cells

And there's more...

The Voltage of the Cell Depends on the Reactivities

The bigger the difference between the reactivity of the metal of the anode and the metal of the cathode, the more electrons move from the anode to the cathode.
That means that the bigger the difference in reactivity, the bigger the voltage of the cell.

Or, looking at it another way, a cell will shift more electrons if it's really easy for the anode to lose electrons and really easy for the cathode to gain electrons.

Standard Electrode Potentials Tell You the Voltage

1) Standard Electrode Potential sounds utterly horrendous, but all it means is "how easy it is for a metal to gain or lose electrons".

2) A list of standard electrode potentials is basically "the reactivity series with numbers".
The more negative the number (or the smaller), the more reactive the element.
For example, the standard electrode potential of lithium is -3.04 volts and that of silver is 0.8 volts — meaning that lithium is more reactive.

3) The potential difference or voltage of an electrochemical cell is equal to the difference in the standard electrode potentials (i.e. you subtract one number from the other to get the voltage of the cell).

4) The cathode (the negative terminal) is the electrode with the most negative standard electrode potential.

EXAMPLE: What's the voltage in a cell made with nickel and lead? Nickel has a standard electrode potential of -0.25 V, and lead has a standard electrode potential of -0.13 V.

STEP 1) Write down the two numbers: -0.13 V and -0.25 V

STEP 2) Subtract the smaller number from the bigger: -0.13 − (-0.25) = +0.12 V

STEP 3) Write down which metal forms which electrode (if you need to):
Since nickel has the more negative standard electrode potential, it'll be the cathode.

Fuel Cells Use Fuel and Oxygen to Make Electricity

1) A fuel cell uses the reaction between a fuel and oxygen to create a voltage. Hydrogen fuel cells are the ones you need to know about.

2) Hydrogen (the fuel) is supplied to the anode, where it gives up electrons (i.e. it's oxidised): $2H_2 \rightarrow 4H^+ + 4e^-$

3) The electrons flow through an external circuit to the cathode — this is the electric current. Also, OH^- ions move from cathode to anode to complete the circuit.

4) At the cathode, oxygen gains the electrons (i.e. it's reduced): $O_2 + 4e^- \rightarrow 2O^{2-}$

5) The overall reaction is $2H_2 + O_2 \rightarrow 2H_2O$.

6) Hydrogen fuel cells are used to provide electrical power in spacecraft such as the Space Shuttle. Some of the product of the reaction (water) is used as drinking water.

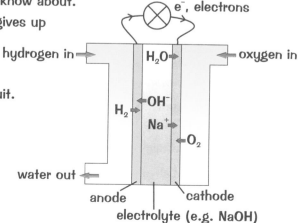

Never mind electrochemical cells — what about my brain cells? Arrgh...

First ask yourself this: "Have I really, really learnt the previous page about electrochemical cells?"
If the answer's "no," then go over that page again. For this page, learn the bit about reactivity and voltage first, then how to do the calculations. Then learn how the hydrogen fuel cell works.

Revision Summary for Section Five

So that's the end of that... another section... all about water and stuff. And what comes next then... well, I guess it's the Chemistry equivalent of extra time. Yep, 12 questions each way (plus an extra question that represents injury time or something). Try the questions without using the book. Then if you got any wrong, go back and have a look at what the answer should have been. And keep doing this forever, or until you can get all the questions right — whichever is the sooner.

1) What's the most common salt present in sea water?

2) Fresh water is slightly acidic. Which gas found in the air causes this acidity, and how?

3) Name four undesirable things that need to be removed from water before it's supplied to homes.

4) What ionic compound is responsible for rusty stains on laundry?

5) What is a colloid?

6) What is a sol? Give an example. Describe two other types of colloid.

7) How do the charges on colloidal particles stop them from sticking together?

8) How do metal ions cause colloids to stick together?

9) Soft water forms a nice foamy lather with soap. What does hard water do with soap?

10) What effect does hard water have on kettles?

11) What salts produce temporary hardness?

12) What salts produce permanent hardness?

13) Name two health benefits of hard water.

14) Which type of hardness is removed by boiling?

15) What is an ion exchange column used for? Explain how they work.

16) What are the products of the electrolysis of molten anhydrous zinc chloride?

17) If 2 amps of current flows for 3 seconds, how much charge is that, in coulombs?

18) What's the name for the amount of charge equal to 1 mole of electrons?
How many coulombs is this?

19) If 3 amps flows for 30 minutes in the electrolysis of copper(II) chloride solution, find:
a) the *mass of copper*, and b) the *volume of chlorine* formed (at STP).

20) At which electrode of a cell is a metal oxidised to a metal ion?

21) Complete the following sentence:
The greater the difference between the reactivities of the metals that the electrodes are made from, the greater the ....

22) If a cell is made with a cathode of magnesium (standard electrode potential -2.38 V) and an anode of tin (standard electrode potential -0.14 V), what voltage is produced?

23) Draw a labelled diagram of a hydrogen fuel cell.

24) Write out the half-equations for a hydrogen fuel cell.

25) What are hydrogen fuel cells used for?

Aluminium and Titanium

Aluminium and titanium are the babes of the metal world.

Aluminium is Reactive, but doesn't Corrode

1) Aluminium is widely used (e.g. in aeroplanes, drinks cans, power cables on pylons, window frames...) because of its low density, good conductivity and corrosion resistance. But it's expensive as it's more reactive than carbon, and so it has to be extracted by electrolysis.

2) Pure aluminium is pretty soft, so it's often alloyed with other metals to make it harder and stronger.

3) A protective layer of unreactive aluminium oxide (Al_2O_3) quickly forms on the surface of aluminium. This is why aluminium doesn't corrode, despite being quite reactive.

The Oxide Layer can be Thickened for Even Greater Protection

1) It's possible to make the surface aluminium oxide layer thicker than it would naturally get — this gives even greater protection for the aluminium underneath.

2) The natural oxide layer is first removed using sodium hydroxide solution.

3) The aluminium is then made the anode of an electrolysis cell, with sulphuric acid as the electrolyte.

4) Oxygen forms on the surface of the aluminium anode, and reacts with the aluminium to form aluminium oxide. This anodising process makes the aluminium even more resistant to corrosion.

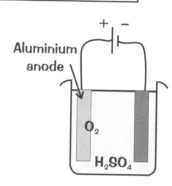
Aluminium anode
O_2
H_2SO_4

$$4OH^- \longrightarrow 2H_2O + O_2 + 4e^-$$

There are some OH^- ions in the acid solution, even though it's an acid. The oxygen forms from these.

Impure Titanium is not much use

1) Titanium is a transition metal — it's better than steel for making most things — and is even more resistant to corrosion than aluminium. Also, its density is low enough for it to be used in aircraft.

2) Its big disadvantage is the cost of extracting it from its ore. Although in theory it's low enough in the reactivity series to be extracted using carbon, carbon impurities in titanium metal make it useless (unlike iron, where a little carbon makes the metal more useful, as it forms steel).

3) In fact, titanium is extracted in an inert atmosphere of argon using a more reactive metal (which first has to be obtained by the expensive process of electrolysis). So titanium turns out to be a very expensive metal.

4) This means it's only used for things where a high cost is justified, such as nuclear reactors, jet engines and replacement hip joints.

Titanium is Extracted using Sodium or Magnesium

1) The main ore of titanium is rutile, TiO_2.

2) Rutile is first converted to titanium chloride, $TiCl_4$.

3) This titanium chloride is then reduced using sodium or magnesium in an argon atmosphere (to prevent contamination), to leave titanium metal.

$$TiCl_4 + 4Na \longrightarrow Ti + 4NaCl$$

Titanium — Queen of fairies and hip joints...

It's easy to remember that aluminium and titanium are dead useful. And it's easy-ish to remember what they're useful for. But it's definitely hard to remember the details about thickening the aluminium oxide layer and extracting titanium. Test how much you remember by writing it all down with the page covered.

Iron, Steel and Alloys

Cast iron from a blast furnace has only limited uses. Although it's very hard and pretty rust-proof, it's also very brittle. But it's good for making products like drain covers.

Steel is an Alloy of Iron and Carbon

1) Steel is a general name given to alloys of iron that contain between 0.05% and 1.5% carbon (and often other metals too).

2) Steels are much more useful than cast iron, but they rust easily.

3) However, there are various ways to prevent steel from rusting so easily (see page 48).

Blast in Oxygen — then get rid of Oxide Impurities

1) The iron produced in a blast furnace is very impure. It contains various impurities such as carbon, manganese, silicon, phosphorus and sulphur.

2) In the first stage of producing steel, impure molten iron from the blast furnace is mixed with scrap iron (this recycling is good for profits and the environment) and, as it is heated, oxygen is blasted through.

3) This converts all the non-metal impurities to oxides. Carbon dioxide (CO_2) and sulphur dioxide (SO_2) come off as gases.

4) Calcium carbonate ($CaCO_3$) is also added — this decomposes to form calcium oxide (CaO) and carbon dioxide.

5) As calcium oxide is basic (it's a metal oxide, after all), it reacts with any non-metal (acidic) oxides, in particular silicon dioxide (SiO_2), to form 'slag'.

6) Calculated amounts of carbon and other metals are then added to give the required alloys.

	Composition	Properties	Uses
Cast iron	4% Carbon	Hard but brittle	Castings of drains, stoves, etc.
High-carbon steel	1.5% Carbon	Very hard	Cutting tools for industry, drill, etc.
Mild steel	0.25% Carbon	Quite soft, shaped 'easily' by pressing	Car bodies, tin cans, girders, etc.
Stainless steels	Contain chromium and/or nickel	Corrosion-resistant and strong	Food vessels, marine and chemical use
Titanium steel	Contains titanium	Very strong	Armour plating, for example
Manganese steel	Contains manganese	Strong, tough, and wear-resistant	Grinding machinery, caterpillar tracks

Brass and Solder are also Alloys

1) Brass is an alloy, usually of copper and zinc. Most of the properties of brass are just a mixture of those of the copper and zinc, although brass is harder than either of them.

2) Solder is an alloy of lead and tin. Unlike pure materials it doesn't have a definite melting point, but gradually solidifies as it cools down. This is pretty useful if you want to solder things together.

Any old iron, any old iron, any any any old iron...

This alloying business is mega-important in the metal industry, because it means a product can be made that has just the properties you want. As for the page, well, it's mostly okay, but getting your head round why using calcium carbonate is a good idea is a little tricky. But get your head round it, you must.

Protecting Iron and Steel

If you don't take care of steel, it'll rust away. And then where will you be... eh... eh...
Sigh... learn this page and you need never find yourself in that kind of situation.

There are loads of ways to Prevent Rusting

Iron and some steels will rust if they come into contact with air and water.
To prevent this, there are various things you can do:

1) Galvanise it (i.e. coat it with a thin layer of zinc, either by
   dipping the iron into molten zinc or by electrolysis),
2) Paint it,
3) Oil or grease it,
4) Use sacrificial protection (i.e. attach a block of a more reactive
   metal to the iron, which corrodes instead of the iron).

Or use a suitable alloy — like stainless steel, for example.

Electroplating means Coating one Metal with Another

Electroplating means using electrolysis to coat one metal with a layer of another.

Say you want to coat an iron teapot with a thin layer of copper, then what you do is this:

1) Use the teapot as the negative electrode (cathode) in an electrolysis cell.
2) Make the anode out of the metal you want to form the coating (in this case, copper).
3) As the electrolyte, you need a solution containing copper ions (or whatever metal you
   want to form the coating), so in this case you could use copper sulphate.

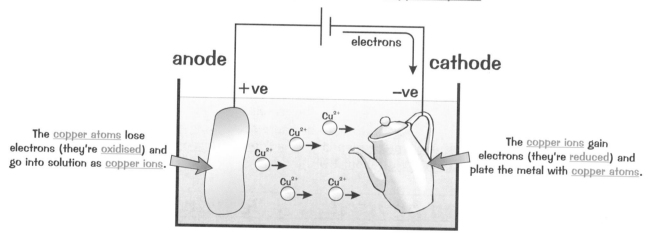

anode   electrons   cathode

+ve   −ve

The copper atoms lose
electrons (they're oxidised) and
go into solution as copper ions.

The copper ions gain
electrons (they're reduced) and
plate the metal with copper atoms.

1) At the anode, electrons are removed from copper atoms, which then go into solution as ions:
   $Cu(s) \longrightarrow Cu^{2+}(aq) + 2e^-$
2) The electrons flow to the teapot (the cathode), attracting $Cu^{2+}(aq)$ ions. These ions accept
   the electrons to form copper atoms, which stick to the teapot: $Cu^{2+}(aq) + 2e^- \longrightarrow Cu(s)$.
3) This all means that the concentration of copper in solution remains constant, but a very thin layer of
   copper deposits on the teapot, and an identical mass is lost from the copper anode. Clever.
4) Gold, silver and nickel plating are done in the same way, but the cations (the positive ions) in solution
   and the anode are gold, silver or nickel (obviously).

Sacrificial protection — sounds dangerous to me...

You may recognise these equations from the Chemistry Revision Guide. The half equations for copper
plating are just the same as the ones for purifying copper by electrolysis — the only difference is
whether you start with a cathode of pure copper or a cathode of another metal.

Sulphuric Acid

Loads of modern industries use tonnes of sulphuric acid, so it's pretty important stuff.
And the good thing is... you need to know how it's made.

The Contact Process is used to make Sulphuric Acid

1) The first stage of the Contact Process involves forming sulphur dioxide (SO_2). This is usually done by burning sulphur in air or roasting sulphide ores. (There are various sulphur deposits around the world, although some SO_2 comes from metal extraction industries — see page 47.)

$$S + O_2 \longrightarrow SO_2$$

2) The sulphur dioxide is then oxidised (with the help of a catalyst) to form sulphur trioxide (SO_3).

$$2SO_2 + O_2 \rightleftharpoons 2SO_3$$

3) Next, the sulphur trioxide is dissolved in concentrated sulphuric acid to form fuming sulphuric acid, or oleum.

Dissolving SO_3 in water doesn't work — the reaction gives out enough heat to evaporate the sulphuric acid.

$$SO_3 + H_2SO_4 \longrightarrow H_2S_2O_7$$

4) Finally, oleum is diluted with measured amounts of water to form concentrated sulphuric acid.

$$H_2S_2O_7 + H_2O \longrightarrow 2H_2SO_4$$

A Catalyst is Important when making SO_3

1) The reaction in step 2 above (oxidising sulphur dioxide to sulphur trioxide) is exothermic (i.e. it gives out heat). Also, there are two moles of product, compared to three moles of reactants.

Conditions for Contact Process

1) Temperature: 450 °C.
2) Pressure: 1-2 atmospheres.
3) Catalyst: Often vanadium pentoxide, V_2O_5 (but others can also be used).

2) So Le Chatelier's principle (see the Chemistry book) says that to get more product, you should reduce the temperature and increase the pressure.

3) Unfortunately, reducing the temperature slows the reaction right down, and increasing the pressure soon liquefies the SO_2 — no use at all.

4) With a fairly high temperature, a low pressure and a vanadium pentoxide catalyst, the reaction goes pretty quickly and you get a good yield (about 99%).

Sulphuric Acid can be used as a Dehydrating Agent

1) Sulphuric acid is used in car batteries (and is concentrated enough to cause severe burns).

2) It's also used in many manufacturing processes, such as making fertilisers and detergents.

3) And sulphuric acid is also a powerful dehydrating agent. It removes hydrogen and oxygen from organic material (like sugar), and things like hydrated copper(II) sulphate (which goes from blue to white as the water of crystallisation is removed).

$$C_6H_{12}O_6 \longrightarrow 6C + 6H_2O$$
glucose (sugar) $\longrightarrow$ carbon + water

$$CuSO_4.5H_2O \longrightarrow CuSO_4 + 5H_2O$$
hydrated copper(II) sulphate $\longrightarrow$ anhydrous copper(II) sulphate + water

Eeuucch... Burning sulphur? — imagine the smell...

This is important stuff (in real life and for Chemistry revision). You need to understand why the catalyst is so vital in the Contact Process. Le Chatelier's principle seems to put loads of obstacles in the way of getting the all-important sulphur trioxide — the catalyst provides a handy way round them.

Homologous Series and Isomers

The rest of this section is about organic chemistry, which is largely to do with 'families' of carbon compounds. The members of each of these families are all pretty similar.

Homologous Series are Families of Carbon Compounds

The members of a homologous series all have certain things in common.

1) They all have the same general formula.

2) They all have similar reactions.

3) They can all be made in similar ways.

> Alkanes and alkenes are examples of homologous series. Alkanes have a general formula of C_nH_{2n+2}, and alkenes have a general formula of C_nH_{2n}.

4) Certain properties change gradually as you go through the series (i.e. as more carbon atoms are added). For example, as the molecules get larger, the melting and boiling points increase.

> The names of the members of many homologous series follow a similar pattern.
> Alkanes: methane (CH_4), ethane (C_2H_6), propane (C_3H_8) and butane (C_4H_{10}).
> Alkenes: ethene (C_2H_4), propene (C_3H_6) and butene (C_4H_8).

Things starting with 'eth-' have 2 carbon atoms, 'prop-' have 3, and so on.

The Functional Group gives a Family its Character

1) The functional group is the characteristic that all members of a homologous series have in common. It's the functional group (or lack of one, in the case of alkanes) that's responsible for each member of that family acting in a similar way.

2) So for alkenes, the functional group is the pair of double-bonded carbon atoms.

3) Alcohols (see page 51) have the functional group -OH.

4) And carboxylic acids (see page 53) have the functional group -COOH.

Isomers have their Atoms Arranged Differently

Organic chemistry is a huge subject. One reason is that the atoms in many compounds can be arranged in different ways. Compounds which have the same formula but different structures are called isomers.

For example — pentane has the formula C_5H_{12}, but the atoms in pentane can be arranged as below:

Isomer 1

H—C—C—C—C—C—H (with H atoms attached)

Isomer 2

H—C—C—C—C—H (branched with CH at bottom)

Isomer 3

branched structure

1) Different isomers often have different physical properties (so things like melting and boiling points might be different, for example).

2) These different properties are because the strengths of the intermolecular bonds depends on the exact arrangement of the atoms.

3) Molecules that are long and thin have higher melting and boiling points than branched molecules.

4) This is because long, thin molecules pack together better, and so have more contact with other molecules. This means that the intermolecular forces are stronger.

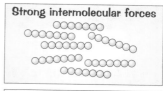
Strong intermolecular forces

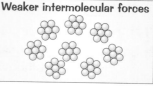
Weaker intermolecular forces

So does that mean the Simpsons are a dysfunctional group...

One good thing about organic chemistry is that it's all about learning patterns and trends. Learn the basics well (like the meth-, eth-, prop-, but- names), and you can keep using the same ol' facts, time and time again. As ever, test yourself by covering the page and writing down as much as you can.

Alcohols

Don't get your hopes up... this page is all about carbon chains with an -OH functional group.
It's the -OH which makes them react as alcohols.

Alcohols have an '-OH' Functional Group and end in '-ol'

The basic naming system is the same as for alkanes — but replace the final '-e' with '-ol'.

Methanol

$$H-C-O-H$$

CH_3OH

Ethanol

$$H-C-C-O-H$$

C_2H_5OH

Propanol

$$H-C-C-C-O-H$$

C_3H_7OH

Butanol

$$H-C-C-C-C-O-H$$

C_4H_9OH

Don't write CH_4O instead of CH_3OH, or C_2H_6O instead of C_2H_5OH, etc.,
as it doesn't show the functional -OH group.

All Alcohols react in a Similar Way

Being members of a homologous series, the reactions of all alcohols are similar.

(1) **Combustion:** All alcohols burn, giving carbon dioxide and water (and heat).

$$2CH_3OH + 3O_2 \longrightarrow 2CO_2 + 4H_2O \qquad C_2H_5OH + 3O_2 \longrightarrow 2CO_2 + 3H_2O$$

(2) **Reaction with sodium:** Alcohols react with sodium metal to give off hydrogen.

$$2C_2H_5OH + 2Na \longrightarrow 2C_2H_5ONa + H_2$$

(3) **Esterification:** Alcohols react with carboxylic acids (see page 53) to form esters (see page 54).

Alcohols are Used as Fuels and Solvents

1) Some alcohols are used as fuels. Ethanol is used as a fuel in 'spirit' burners — it burns cleanly, is non-smelly and washes off with water. In fact, some countries that have little or no oil deposits but plenty of sunshine (e.g. Brazil) grow loads of sugar cane, which they ferment to form ethanol (see pages 14 and 52). This can then be added to petrol.

2) Ethanol (as well as some other alcohols) is used as a solvent. 'Methylated spirit' (or 'meths') is mainly ethanol, but it has methanol added to it to make it 'undrinkable', and a blue dye to stop people drinking it by mistake. It's used to clean paint brushes.

Cholesterol contains the Alcohol Group -OH

1) Cholesterol contains the alcohol functional group -OH.
2) It belongs to the group of compounds known as steroids.
3) Cholesterol is essential to your body chemistry. Your body produces it, but if excess amounts are present, it's thought to contribute to heart disease.

OH-OH — It's the page all about alcohols...

Let me guess... you're trying to work out how many allotments you'd need in order to be able to grow enough sugar cane so that you'd never have to buy any petrol ever. Well, let me tell you something — it's quite a few. And there are all sorts of problems in practice. Trust me on this, I tried it.

Ethanol

Ethanol has been known since ancient times. Explains why there are so many ancient ruins, I guess. They were always too drunk to finish the job properly.

Make Ethanol by Fermentation or Hydration of Ethene

① **FERMENTATION** — Ethanol has been made by fermentation for thousands of years.

1) The process of fermentation converts sugars (usually from fruits and vegetables) into ethanol.

$$C_6H_{12}O_6 \longrightarrow 2C_2H_5OH + 2CO_2$$

See the Biology book for more info about enzymes.

2) The reaction is brought about by enzymes (naturally occurring catalysts) found in yeasts, and goes quickest at about 30 °C (if it gets too hot the enzymes are destroyed).

3) During fermentation, it's important to prevent oxygen getting at the alcohol. This is because oxygen converts ethanol to ethanoic acid (which is what you get in vinegar). It's also because if oxygen is present, the yeast respires aerobically to produce just carbon dioxide and water (see page 2).

4) When the concentration of alcohol reaches about 10-15%, the reaction stops, due to the yeast being killed by the alcohol. (Spirits are made by distilling already fermented brews.)

② **HYDRATION OF ALKENES** — this is how alcohols are commonly made industrially.
Ethene, made during the cracking of crude oil (see Chemistry book), will react with steam at 300 °C and a pressure of 70 atmospheres, using phosphoric acid as a catalyst. The product is ethanol.

These Methods have their Pros and Cons

	Fermentation	Hydration of Ethene
Advantages	1. Low tech 2. Uses a renewable resource	1. High quality product 2. Quick 3. Efficient, as process runs continuously
Disadvantages	1. Expensive to concentrate and purify 2. Fermentation is slow 3. Made in batches (i.e. process can't be left to run continuously, so less efficient)	1. Requires large chemical plant 2. Ethene is a finite resource

Ethanol is used to make Ethene and in Alcoholic Drinks

To make ethene
i) The plastics and polymer industries use lots of ethene.

ii) Countries which have no oil but plenty of land for growing crops for fermentation can make ethene through the dehydration of ethanol, using a heated aluminium oxide catalyst. (The reaction is the exact opposite of the one in the second blue box above.)

In drink Alcoholic drinks contain ethanol. Beers contain around 3-6% ethanol, wines about 9-15%. Spirits like whisky, gin and brandy are made by the fractional distillation of wines and other fermented brews. The distilled liquid has a higher percentage of alcohol, usually around 40%.

In vino, veritas — yep, this stuff about ethanol is all true...

Hmm, at the top it says you make ethanol from ethene, and then later on it says you make ethene from ethanol. It all comes down to what you've got more of — if you've got oil and need ethanol, you do one thing. But if you've got easy access to ethanol and need ethene, you do the other. Makes sense.

Carboxylic Acids

So what if carboxylic is a funny name... these beauties make for an easy topic.

Carboxylic Acids have Functional Group -COOH

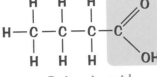

1) Carboxylic acids have '-COOH' as a functional group.

2) They are weak acids — less than 1% of the molecules ionise in water.

e.g. ethanoic acid: $CH_3COOH(l) \rightleftharpoons CH_3COO^-(aq) + H^+(aq)$

3) Their names end in '-anoic acid' (and start with the normal 'meth/eth/prop/but').

Methanoic acid   Ethanoic acid   Propanoic acid   Butanoic acid

Carboxylic Acids react like other Acids

Carboxylic acids... well, they're acids. And they do normal acid things:

1) With metals they form salts and hydrogen:

$$2CH_3COOH + Mg \longrightarrow H_2 + Mg^{2+}(CH_3COO^-)_2$$

The salts are ethanoates — e.g. magnesium ethanoate.

2) With carbonates (CO_3^{2-}) and hydrogencarbonates (HCO_3^-) they form salts, carbon dioxide and water:

$$Na_2CO_3 + 2CH_3COOH \longrightarrow 2Na^+CH_3COO^- + CO_2 + H_2O$$

$$Mg(HCO_3)_2 + 2HCOOH \longrightarrow Mg^{2+}(HCOO^-)_2 + 2CO_2 + 2H_2O$$

3) With alkalis they are neutralised:

$$H^+ + OH^- \longrightarrow H_2O$$

This is the ionic equation for a neutralisation reaction — the H+ represents the acid, the OH− represents the alkali.

4) With indicators they give typical acid colours:

Universal indicator goes orange / red.   Phenolphthalein is colourless.

Some Carboxylic Acids are Fairly Common

1) Ethanoic acid is the acid in vinegar, which is used for flavouring and preserving foods.

2) If wine or beer is left open to the air, the ethanol is oxidised to ethanoic acid. This is why drinking wine after it's been open for a couple of days is like drinking vinegar — basically it is vinegar.

$$\text{ethanol} + \text{oxygen} \longrightarrow \text{vinegar} + \text{water}$$
$$CH_3CH_2OH + O_2 \longrightarrow CH_3COOH + H_2O$$

3) Ethanoic acid is also used in the manufacture of rayon, a synthetic fibre.

4) Citric acid is present in oranges and lemons, and is manufactured in large quantities to make fizzy drinks. It's also used as a descaler (see page 41 about hard water).

5) Aspirin is a man-made carboxylic acid. It's not only an analgesic (painkiller), but it reduces blood clotting slightly, and is regularly taken by people at risk of heart attack.

COOH — what a fantastic page about acids...

You should also know a little about ascorbic acid (vitamin C). Ascorbic acid is in loads of green vegetables, oranges and tomatoes, and so on. It's dead important for human health in loads of ways — so you should always do as my mum says and make sure you eat your greens. Or else...

Esters

It's the topic you've been waiting for... esters. This page may not change your life exactly, but by the time you've read it through to the end, you'll know what makes those nice pear-drop sweets smell.

Alcohol + Acid ⟶ Ester + Water

1) Esters are formed from an alcohol and a carboxylic acid. This process is called esterification.

2) An acid catalyst is usually used (e.g. concentrated sulphuric acid).

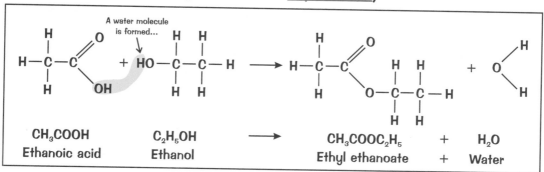

CH$_3$COOH   C$_2$H$_5$OH   ⟶   CH$_3$COOC$_2$H$_5$ + H$_2$O

Ethanoic acid   Ethanol   Ethyl ethanoate + Water

Learn what you get with other Alcohols and Carboxylic Acids

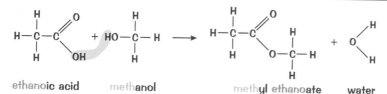

ethanoic acid   methanol   methyl ethanoate   water

1) The alcohol forms the first part of the ester's name.

2) The acid forms the second part.

Esterification is Reversible

1) The above process is reversible — an ester reacts with water to form an alcohol and a carboxylic acid.

2) This process is called ester hydrolysis.

Esters are often used in Flavourings and Perfumes

1) Esters have quite strong smells, though these are usually quite pleasant.

2) Esters are pretty common in nature. Loads of common food smells (plus those in products like perfumes) contain natural esters.

3) Esters are also manufactured synthetically to enhance food flavours or aromas, e.g. there are esters that smell of rum, apple, orange, pineapple, and so on. And esters are responsible for the distinctive smell of pear-drops.

4) Other esters are the basis of familiar smells in drinks, glues, paints and ointments (e.g. that lovely Deep-Heat smell).

5) And the formation of natural esters in wines and spirits gives a pleasant aroma to these drinks, and removes a lot of the acids (that are partly responsible for the hangover headaches).

Mmmm... pear-drops...

So now you know the answer to the burning question of what makes pear-drops smell the way they do. It's all down to esters. And polyesters (as if you couldn't guess) are things made from lots of ester molecules. So if someone asks you the chemical formula of a pair of trousers, you can tell them.

Free Radicals

Free radicals — sounds like someone calling for dissident political prisoners to be freed. But it isn't...

Free Radicals are Made by Breaking Covalent Bonds

1) A covalent bond, remember, is one where two atoms share electrons between them, like in H_2.

2) A covalent bond can break unevenly to form two ions, e.g. $H–H \rightarrow H^+ + H^-$. The H^- has both of the shared electrons, and the poor old H^+ has neither of them.

3) But a covalent bond can also break evenly — and then each atom gets one of the shared electrons, e.g. $H–H \rightarrow H· + H·$ — the $H·$ is called a free radical. (A free radical is shown by a dot.)

4) The free radical has one electron out of a pair, and so it's very, very reactive.

Chlorofluorocarbons contain Chlorine and Fluorine

1) Chlorofluorocarbons (CFCs for short) are organic molecules containing chlorine and fluorine, e.g. dichlorodifluoromethane CCl_2F_2, which is like methane but with two chlorine and two fluorine atoms (and an extremely long name) instead of the four hydrogen atoms.

2) Chlorofluorocarbons were used as coolants in refrigerators and air-conditioning systems.

3) CFCs were also used as propellants in aerosol spray cans.

Free Radicals from CFCs Damage the Ozone Layer

1) Ultraviolet light makes CFCs break up to form free radicals: $CCl_2F_2 \rightarrow CClF_2· + Cl·$

2) This happens high up in the atmosphere, where the ultraviolet light from the Sun is stronger.

3) Chlorine free radicals react with ozone (O_3), turning it into ordinary oxygen molecules (O_2):

$$O_3 + Cl· \rightarrow ClO + O_2$$

4) The chlorine oxide molecule ClO is very reactive, and reacts with any oxygen atoms around to make an oxygen molecule and another Cl· free radical.

$$ClO + O \rightarrow O_2 + Cl·$$

5) Because a chlorine free radical gets regenerated each time, one free radical can go around breaking up a lot of ozone molecules. So it's bye-bye ozone layer.

The Ozone Layer Shields the Earth from UV light

Because the ozone layer has been damaged by chlorine free radicals, more ultraviolet light reaches the Earth's surface. Ultraviolet light is harmful to living things — in people it causes:

i) Sunburn, ii) Premature aging of the skin, iii) Skin cancer.

CFCs are Banned in Some Countries

In many countries of the world CFC manufacture is banned. Butane is used as a propellant in aerosols instead of CFCs, and old fridges that contain CFCs have to be specially dealt with so that CFCs don't escape.

But getting agreement between all the countries of the world to ban the manufacture and use of harmful materials is difficult.

Free radicals — I'm telling you... they ain't done nothing...

Lots of new stuff, but all you have to do is learn the subsections one by one. First, learn what free radicals are, and what chlorofluorocarbons are. Then learn what they do to the ozone layer. Then the three ways that UV light damages living things, and learn the stuff about banning CFCs. Simple.

Revision Summary for Section Six

Quite a mixed bag of stuff in that section. Reasonably interesting too. Without this, there'd be no drinks in cans or plastic bottles, no transport, no communications... in fact without chemistry we'd still be in the Stone Age (or thereabouts). Anyway, fascinated by industrial chemistry or not, you've still gotta learn it. These questions are all perfectly tailored to help you check what you know and what you don't.

1) Why might it be beneficial to get a thicker oxide layer on the surface of aluminium?
2) What is used to remove the aluminium oxide layer prior to making a new one?
3) Name the electrolyte used in the process of "anodising" aluminium.
4) In what way is titanium more useful than aluminium?
5) Is titanium above or below carbon in the reactivity series?
   Why isn't titanium oxide reduced with carbon?
6) In the extraction of titanium from rutile (TiO_2), what is rutile converted into before it is reduced?
7) Balance the equation for the reduction of titanium chloride with magnesium:
   $Mg + TiCl_4 \rightarrow MgCl_2 + Ti$.
8) Draw a table to compare the composition, main properties and main uses of the following metals: cast iron, high carbon steel, mild steel and stainless steel(s).
9) Name two other alloys and state their constituent metals.
10) In the first stage of producing steel, what is removed from the molten iron by blowing oxygen through it? Explain how this works.
11) What happens when limestone is added to the molten iron?
12) Name four different methods used to protect iron and steel from corrosion.
13) In order to plate a copper item with nickel in an electrolysis cell, what should be used for
    a) the anode, and b) the cathode? c) Name a suitable electrolyte.
14) What is the "Contact Process" used to make? Describe the process in detail, including equations.
15) What is a dehydrating agent? What are the products of the reaction between concentrated sulphuric acid and sugar?
16) What would be similar about all the members of a homologous series of carbon compounds?
17) What are 'isomers'? Draw three isomers of pentane, C_5H_{12}.
18) Describe how one physical property of these three isomers is affected by the different arrangement of atoms.
19) What do all alcohols have in common?
20) Balance these equations: a) $C_3H_7OH + O_2 \rightarrow CO_2 + H_2O$ and b) $Na + C_2H_5OH \rightarrow C_2H_5ONa + H_2$
21) Describe two uses of alcohols.
22) Why is too much cholesterol bad for you?
23) Describe two commercial ways of making ethanol.
    List two advantages and two disadvantages of each method.
24) Describe two uses of ethanol.
25) What is the functional group of carboxylic acids?
    Draw the structure of the first four carboxylic acids.
26) Write an equation for ethanoic acid reacting with a) magnesium, and b) sodium hydrogencarbonate.
27) Name two "everyday" places where ethanoic acid might be found.
28) Draw the structure of methyl ethanoate. Write an equation for its formation.
29) State one important property of esters.
30) How are free radicals formed?
31) How many free (unpaired) electrons does a free radical have?
32) What is a chlorofluorocarbon?
33) What were (or are) chlorofluorocarbons used for?
34) What happens to chlorofluorocarbons in the upper atmosphere?
35) What kind of free radical is mainly responsible for depletion of the ozone layer?
36) Name three health dangers that result from the depletion of the ozone layer?

Carbohydrates

The three major nutrients in food are carbohydrates, protein and fats.
And it's the carbohydrates that give us most of our energy.

Carbohydrates — made of Carbon, Hydrogen and Oxygen

1) Carbohydrates consist of carbon (C), hydrogen (H) and oxygen (O).
They all have the general formula:

$$C_x(H_2O)_y$$

There are always twice as many hydrogens as there are oxygens.

2) Glucose, sucrose, starch and cellulose are all carbohydrates.

Two Monosaccharides Join to make a Disaccharide

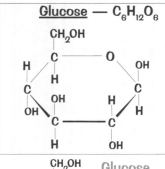

Glucose — $C_6H_{12}O_6$

1) Small soluble carbohydrates are called sugars, e.g. glucose.

2) Glucose is a monosaccharide — it's made of a single sugar unit — this sugar unit is a ring-shaped molecule.

3) When two monosaccharides bond together a disaccharide is formed — it has two rings.

4) The monosaccharides glucose and fructose join to form sucrose — a disaccharide. This is called a condensation reaction because a water molecule is produced as the two molecules join.

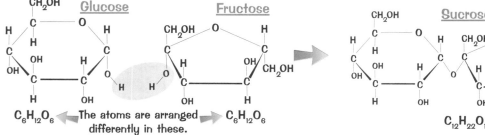

Glucose   Fructose   Sucrose — a disaccharide   + H_2O

$C_6H_{12}O_6$ ← The atoms are arranged → $C_6H_{12}O_6$ $C_{12}H_{22}O_{11}$
differently in these.

Polysaccharides are Polymers of Monosaccharides

1) Monosaccharides join together in long chains to form polysaccharides.

2) Polysaccharides form by condensation polymerisation — a water molecule is produced for every monosaccharide that joins on.

3) Starch and cellulose are polysaccharides — they are polymers of glucose.

4) You need to be able to draw the outline structural formulae for starch and cellulose.
Starch is easy to draw — just a simple chain of glucose molecules.
Cellulose is pretty similar, except alternate glucose molecules are flipped over.

Starch   Cellulose

I can't make it any sweeter for you — you just have to learn it...

The worst thing about this page is all the structures you need to learn — cover the page and draw glucose, sucrose, starch and cellulose. Keep trying 'til you get them spot on. The rest of the page is pretty logical.
Carbohydrates are made of carbon and water (H_2O) — hydrate always means there's water involved.

Proteins and Fats

Amino acids are pretty useful — they make up proteins, which we need to make new cells and to grow.

Amino Acids have a -COOH Group and an -NH₂ Group

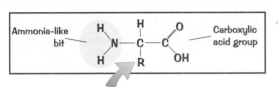

1) Amino acids are easy to recognise.
They always contain a carboxylic acid group -COOH and an ammonia-like bit -NH₂ (an amine group).

R can be pretty much anything — an H atom, a chain of carbon atoms...

2) The simplest amino acid is glycine — it has two hydrogens on the central carbon.

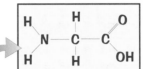

Proteins are Polymers of Amino Acids

1) Ammonia reacts with acids — so the ammonia-like bit at the end of one amino acid molecule will react with the carboxylic acid bit at the end of another amino acid molecule.

2) In this way, loads of amino acids join together to form a polymer. Polymers of amino acids are called polypeptides or proteins.

3) This reaction is called condensation polymerisation because a water molecule forms as the amino acids join together. This is just like the formation of polysaccharides (see page 57).

Peptide links join one amino acid to the next — that's why the chains are called polypeptides. (See also page 16.)

Polymers are long chains of small molecules.

Peptide link

Triglycerides are Esters made from Glycerol

1) Triglycerides are fats or oils.

2) They're esters made from glycerol — an alcohol with 3 -OH groups.

Example:

Glycerol   Carboxylic acid   Triglyceride

R is a long carbon chain here

See Section 6 for more about alcohols, carboxylic acids and esters.

Big Molecules can be Broken Down by Hydrolysis

1) Reactions which form polypeptides, triglycerides and polysaccharides (see page 57) also form water.

2) These reactions are all reversible. With water, the big molecules slowly revert to small molecules.

Hydrolysis (with water)

Polypeptides ⟹ Amino acids

Triglycerides ⟹ Glycerol + carboxylic acid

Polysaccharides ⟹ Monosaccharides

Well, aminos — that's all there is to it...

Polypeptides, polysaccharides — there must be a parrot joke in here somewhere.
Make sure you can spot an amino acid from a mile away, even if its cunningly disguised as a coco-pop.
As for the triglyceride molecule — you'd better get on with memorising that one. Go on then.

<u>Diet</u>

<u>A Balanced Diet is Important for Good Health</u>

1) A <u>balanced</u> diet provides <u>all</u> the stuff our bodies need. Different people need <u>different</u> diets.

2) The more <u>active</u> you are the more energy you need. Children need more <u>energy</u> and <u>protein</u> than an adult of the same size would need. <u>Adolescents</u> are <u>growing</u> quickly and need <u>lots</u> of food too. <u>Pregnant</u> and <u>breast-feeding</u> women need <u>extra</u> food for the baby as well as themselves.

3) A balanced diet <u>must</u> contain the correct amounts of the following:

<u>Fats</u> and <u>Carbohydrates</u> provide Energy

1) Fats and carbohydrates provide <u>energy</u> to <u>move</u> and keep <u>warm</u>.

2) Too much sugar (a carbohydrate) leads to <u>tooth decay</u>.

3) <u>Fats</u> can be <u>saturated</u> or <u>unsaturated</u>.

4) Unsaturated fats come from <u>plants</u> and have C=C double bonds in their carbon chains.

5) Saturated fats come mainly from <u>animals</u> and have <u>no</u> C=C double bonds. Eating excessive <u>saturated</u> fat increases the risk of <u>heart disease</u>.

Making Margarine

1) <u>Unsaturated</u> vegetable oils are used to make <u>margarine</u>.

2) A <u>nickel catalyst</u> can make some <u>double</u> bonds break and accept <u>hydrogen</u> atoms. The oil then becomes a <u>solid</u> fat (hydrogenated vegetable oil).

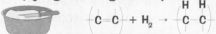

<u>Protein</u> — for Energy and Growth

1) Protein's needed for <u>growth</u>, and <u>cell repair</u> and <u>replacement</u>.

2) You need to eat certain <u>amino acids</u> so that your body can make <u>other</u> amino acids it needs.

3) <u>Vegetarians</u> must be careful to eat enough protein to make sure they get the amino acids which our bodies <u>can't</u> make.

<u>Fibre</u> — Indigestible Carbohydrate

1) Fibre is mainly <u>cellulose</u> from plants.

2) It keeps food <u>moving</u> smoothly through your digestive system by providing something for your gut muscles to <u>push</u> against.

<u>Vitamins</u> and <u>Minerals</u> are needed in Tiny Amounts

<u>Vitamin A</u>: For making pigment in the <u>eye</u>.

<u>Vitamin C</u>: Keeps the <u>skin</u> strong and supple. Prevents <u>scurvy</u> (a nutritional disease). Protects <u>tissues</u> by destroying harmful free radicals (see page 55). Vitamin C Levels are reduced by <u>storing</u> food for too long or <u>overcooking</u> it.

<u>Vitamin D</u>: Needed for strong <u>bones</u> and <u>teeth</u>.

<u>Calcium</u>: For healthy <u>bones</u> and <u>teeth</u>.

<u>Iron</u>: For making <u>haemoglobin</u> in red blood cells.

<u>Raising Agents</u> make Bread and Cakes Rise when Cooked

1) Cakes and bread <u>rise</u> when cooked — gases trapped inside the ingredients <u>expand</u> when heated.

2) When baking bread, <u>carbon dioxide</u> is produced by <u>yeast</u> fermenting the sugar (see p52).

3) <u>Baking soda</u> is a mixture of sodium hydrogencarbonate and tartaric acid. It releases <u>carbon dioxide</u> when it becomes wet.

<u>Additives</u> are Chemicals added to Food

1) The <u>E-number</u> system is a list of permitted food additives. Some are <u>natural</u> but most are <u>man-made</u>.

2) Some additives <u>don't</u> have any effect on you, e.g. E175 — gold, while some are <u>beneficial</u>, e.g. E300 — vitamin C. Others can be <u>harmful</u>, e.g. salt contributes to high blood pressure. Some people try to avoid foods with certain additives in.

<u>Colourings</u> — Improve appearance of food, e.g. E160b (Annatto, a yellow dye).
<u>Flavourings</u> — Improve taste, e.g. MSG.
<u>Preservatives</u> — Makes food last longer, e.g. E220, Sulphur dioxide.
<u>Sweeteners</u> — Food can taste sweet without being so fattening, e.g. Nutrasweet.

<u>Food glorious food — hot sausage and mustard...</u>

You need to know <u>what</u> you need and <u>why</u> you need it. Make sure you know the difference between <u>unsaturated</u> fat and the evil, artery clogging, <u>saturated</u> kind. You know the drill — <u>learn</u> the headings, shut the book and see what you can write down. Then <u>check</u> back, and see what you missed.

Drugs

Drugs aren't just things you're told to say no to — they're anything which alters your body's chemistry. Drugs can be dangerous, but some cure people of conditions which would have killed them in the past.

Drugs affect Chemical Reactions in the Body

1) Drugs are things we take which change chemical reactions in the body.

2) For example, analgesics are drugs used to reduce pain, e.g. aspirin, paracetamol and ibuprofen.

Aspirin isn't a Recent Invention

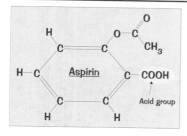

1) Aspirin is used to relieve pain and reduce fever. It can also stop blood clots forming, and so reduce the danger of heart attacks and strokes.

2) The Greeks used white willow bark to reduce pain — the problem was it also caused vomiting. The painkilling ingredient was salicylic acid — and in 1893, a German scientist made a similar chemical which had fewer side effects. This drug is known as aspirin.

3) Aspirin is now the largest selling drug in the world.

Soluble Aspirin Works Faster than Normal Aspirin

1) Aspirin works at the site of an injury by stopping prostaglandin being made. Prostaglandin is a chemical which causes swelling and is involved in the feeling of pain.

2) Aspirin molecules are not very soluble so they get to the injury slowly.

3) But since aspirin is an acid, it reacts with sodium carbonate to form a soluble salt. This salt is the soluble form of aspirin and gets into the blood more quickly. Hurrah.

New Drugs are Extensively Tested

1) Modern drugs now cure illnesses that were once fatal — but there are still diseases with no known cure.

2) Constant research is done to find new and better drugs.

3) Extensive testing is done on potential new drugs in controlled experiments with many stages. Only drugs which pass one stage continue to the next.

> STAGES OF DRUG TESTING
> 1) The drug is tested on cells growing in a tissue culture.
> 2) Next it is tested on laboratory animals, such as rats — many people object to animal testing.
> 3) If the drugs have the desired effect, human trials start.
>   Phase 1 — A small group (less than 100) volunteers.
>   Phase 2 — A larger group of patients (several hundred).
>   Phase 3 — A very large group of patients (tens of thousands).

4) At each stage extensive observation and recording of results is done.

5) The results are compared against established drugs and placebos (fake drugs that have no physical effect) in double blind tests — neither the patients or researchers know who took which pills until later.

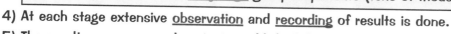

A patient can sometimes get better because they believe they're being treated (even when they're not). A placebo is used as a comparison to the drug being tested.

6) A recent trial was stopped when it became obvious that the drug being tested was having a positive effect — it was thought wrong to carry on using placebos when a successful drug had been found.

There's no aspirin in the jungle — parrots eat 'em all...

The aspirin molecule — yet another structure to learn... that's chemistry for you. Don't you just love it. Make sure you know what drugs are and that analgesic is just a posh name for painkiller. Remember — soluble aspirin is the salt formed by aspirin and sodium carbonate and works faster than ordinary aspirin.

Revision Summary for Section Seven

The truth isn't really out there — that was all a lie put about by shady TV execs to make you watch their new series. No, you see the truth is actually here... in this book. On this very page, in fact. And it's time to face up to it. Yes, the moment of truth has finally arrived — in the shape of this revision summary. Try these questions and make sure you really know your stuff by checking your answers against the section. It's the only way to find out how much you really know. And more importantly, how much you don't know.

1) Which elements are carbohydrates made from?
2) Give four examples of carbohydrates.
3) Name and draw a monosaccharide.
4) Name and draw a disaccharide.
5) What are polymers of monosaccharides called?
6) Draw outline structures for starch and cellulose.
7) What two chemical groups do all amino acid molecules have?
8) Draw glycine, the simplest amino acid.
9) When amino acids polymerise, what are the polymers called?
10) What type of reaction occurs when amino acids join together? Why is it called this?
11) What type of compound is made when glycerol reacts with carboxylic acid? Draw this compound.
12) What is hydrolysis?
13) Name three types of compound that undergo hydrolysis.
14) Name two groups of people that may require slightly different diets.
15) How are vegetable oils converted into margarine?
16) Where do unsaturated fats come from?
17) Do unsaturated fats have C=C double bonds?
18) What health problem is eating too much saturated fat linked to?
19) Why do vegetarians have to be more careful about their diet than non-vegetarians?
20) Fibre is indigestible, so why do we need to eat it?
21) Why do we need the following?
     a) Vitamin A   b) Vitamin C   c) Vitamin D   d) Calcium   e) Iron
22) What makes bread and cakes rise?
23) Give four reasons why additives are added to food.
24) What is a drug?
25) What's another word for 'painkiller'?
26) Name three common painkillers.
27) Apart from relieving pain and fever, what is aspirin used for?
28) "Aspirin was invented only 20 years ago." True or false?
29) Draw a molecule of aspirin.
30) Why does plain aspirin take so long to start working? What is sometimes used instead?
31) Describe the three main phases of drug testing.
32) What is a placebo?
33) What are 'double blind' tests?

Dealing with Information

Information can be sent very quickly over long distances in loads of different ways.
There's radio, television, fax, email, the Internet... the list is virtually endless.

Analogue Signals are Different from Digital Ones

1) An analogue quantity can take any value between set limits,
   e.g. the length of an adult's foot could be anything between, say, 150 mm and 300 mm.

2) A digital quantity has a value from a set number of levels,
   e.g. an adult's shoe size can only have set levels e.g. size 4 or size 9½ but not 5¾.

Records are Analogue, CDs are Digital

1) **RECORDS — ANALOGUE STORAGE** Records are flat discs of plastic with a narrow groove starting at the edge and spiralling into the centre. Information is stored as bumps in the groove — the louder the sound, the bigger the bump and the higher the frequency, the closer together the bumps. A needle tracks the groove and responds to the bumps, creating an electrical signal that passes to an amplifier and loudspeaker. A scratch on the track causes disruption to the music.

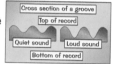

2) **COMPACT DISC (CD) — DIGITAL STORAGE** CDs are reflective discs that have digital data stored as pits (representing 0s) or bumps (representing 1s) in a continuous groove spiralling from the centre of the disc. A laser beam (produced by a diode laser) is moved across the surface of the disk — and the length of the reflected beam is read by a photo-diode detector as 0s and 1s.

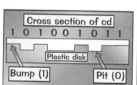
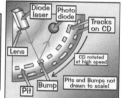

Like records, the music is recorded in sequence, but more information is stored as error correction codes — which enables the CD player to 'guess' what information was destroyed by the scratch.

3) **OPTICAL FIBRES — USED TO SEND DIGITAL INFORMATION**
Once information has been digitally coded (as 0s and 1s), it can be sent down optical fibres. The information is carried as a series of pulses of infrared electromagnetic radiation. Although copper cables can also carry digital signals, optical fibres have the following advantages: greater information capacity, lighter, signals more secure, less subject to noise and travel further before needing amplification or regeneration.

Digital Storage and Transmission is More Convenient...

1) Digital storage mediums only require two states for storage — 0 and 1. The transmitter need only produce two different values. A receiver likewise only needs to recognise these two values.

2) During transmission a signal will get weaker the further it has to travel — this is attenuation. Repeater stations at regular intervals amplify the signal but they can introduce distortion and noise.
Using a regenerator can restore the wave shape of a digital signal.

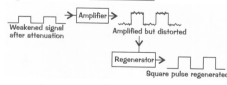

3) Signals are subject to random noise — we hear it as hiss. Noise can add to an analogue signal but is very hard to remove, because the system can't distinguish the noise from the original signal. A digital signal can be 'cleaned' of noise. As long as the noise is not enough for the system to mistake a 0 for a 1, or vice versa, the 0s and 1s will be read correctly.

Groovy baby...

Wheee... — the digital revolution summarised in a page (I'm quite exhausted now). You need to know all the key points about each of the three subheadings. And the diagrams too — learn and scribble...

Radio Waves

Just imagine — if we didn't have radio, there'd be no Top 40, no Evening Session, no Sara Cox... er.. um...

Marconi was the first DJ... (kinda)

Once we'd got <u>bored of shouting</u>, lighting signal fires, writing letters and using carrier pigeons, we started sending <u>telegraphs</u> (or telegrams) — and eventually <u>telephone calls</u> via wires.

Then in 1901, a guy called Guglielmo <u>Marconi</u> demonstrated how to send signals using <u>radio waves</u> across the <u>Atlantic</u> Ocean. These 'wireless' transmissions lead to the development of radio and TV.

More recently such information has been sent very quickly around the world via <u>satellite communications</u>.

Communication Systems *have Eight Parts...*

Communication systems can be broken down into eight blocks, each having specific functions:

1) *ENCODER* <u>converts information</u> into a suitable form for <u>transmission</u>.

2) *MODULATOR* can be used to <u>encode information</u> onto a steady high frequency <u>carrier wave</u>. Amplitude (AM), frequency (FM) or phase (PM) modulation are commonly used.

3) *AMPLIFIER* <u>amplifies</u> the signal before transmission, after reception and before passing to a transducer (like a loudspeaker). This has to occur with the minimum of distortion to the signal to reduce loss of information.

4) *TRANSMITTER* <u>produces the signal</u> that actually <u>travels through the air</u>, along a wire or through an optical fibre. In the case of wireless transmission it involves an aerial.

5) *RECEIVER* <u>accepts the signal</u> sent by the transmitter. It can be an aerial, or it can be at the other end of a wire or optical fibre.

6) *DECODER* takes the received coded signal and <u>extracts the information</u> from it. If the signal contained a <u>modulated</u> carrier wave then a <u>demodulator</u> is used to obtain the original signal from it.

7) *TRANSDUCER* a device that <u>transforms energy</u> from one form to another, often used at the beginning and at the end of an information system.
E.g. a microphone converts a sound wave into an electrical signal ready for encoding. Once the signal has been encoded, sent, received and decoded it can be converted back to sound using a loudspeaker.

8) *STORAGE SYSTEM* e.g. CD, hard drive, magnetic tape etc. — if the information needs to be <u>recorded</u>.

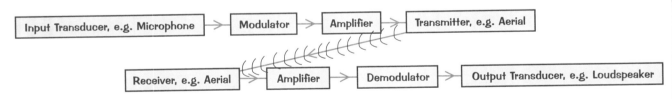

AM *and* FM *are Ways of* Transmitting Radio *Signals*

A <u>radio transmitter</u> sends out a <u>continuous high frequency radio carrier wave</u>.
The <u>signal</u> (e.g. music) is <u>imposed</u> or <u>encoded</u> on the carrier wave in one of two ways:

1) **AM — Amplitude Modulation** The <u>sound wave</u> from the music 'modulates' or <u>changes the carrier wave</u> by <u>changing its amplitude</u>. <u>AM signals</u> have a <u>longer range than FM</u> signals.

2) **FM — Frequency Modulation** The <u>sound wave</u> from the music 'modulates' the <u>carrier wave</u> by <u>changing its frequency</u>. <u>FM radio</u> gives a <u>higher quality sound than AM</u> as the signals are <u>less</u> susceptible to <u>noise and interference</u>.

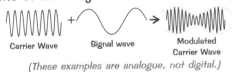

Good old Marconi — what a brain wave...

Main things to remember here are those <u>8 bits of a communication system</u> (and what they do) and how <u>AM</u> and <u>FM</u> are different from each other. Learn the stuff, turn the page, scribble it down.

Radio Waves

This page covers the nuts and bolts of how radio waves are transmitted. Well, not literally the nuts and bolts — this isn't a Resistant Materials book. Although we do have one of those if you want one.

Learn how AM Radio gets from Studio to Kitchen...

You could get a question like: "Describe what happens between the radio DJ speaking in the studio and you hearing their voice coming out of your kitchen radio." And this will be your answer...

1) The sound wave from the DJ's voice is converted into an electrical signal of the same frequency by a microphone.

2) This electrical signal modulates the amplitude (see page 63) of a carrier wave produced by the transmitter. (The carrier wave frequency is specific to that radio station, e.g. 430 kHz for Radio 5.)

3) The transmitter aerial sends the modulated carrier wave out in all directions. This is a high frequency radio wave that travels at the speed of light.

4) Your radio has an aerial that receives the modulated carrier wave and it becomes an electrical signal again. You tune your radio to that particular carrier wave frequency from the hundreds of radio waves from other stations.

5) A diode in the radio removes half of the modulated carrier wave.

6) A capacitor (see page 81) 'filters' out the carrier wave, leaving the original signal from the DJ's voice. This completes the 'demodulation'.

7) An amplifier increases the strength of the signal, then it's converted back to a sound wave in the speaker.

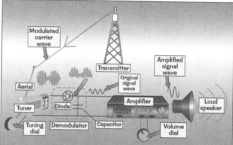

Different Frequency Waves travel via Different Routes

Radio signals can travel to us via different routes, depending on their frequency.

1) **GROUND WAVES** travel in close contact with the ground as they spread out from the transmitter. They travel further over sea than land due to the conductivity of water. Used by LW/MW radio bands (up to 3 MHz).

2) **SKY WAVES** Frequencies up to about 30 MHz (shortwave radio) can reflect off a layer of the atmosphere called the ionosphere. This allows the wave to travel longer distances and deals with the curvature of the Earth. Frequencies above 30 MHz (FM radio and TV) pass straight through the atmosphere and transmissions must be by line of sight.

3) **SPACE WAVES** Microwave signals have a very high carrier frequency (over 3000 MHz for satellite TV and telephones). These pass easily through the atmosphere and reflect off satellites orbiting the Earth enabling the signal to reach distant parts of the planet. Some satellites are passive, simply reflecting signal waves that hit them. Others are active, sending out signals of their own — e.g. weather monitoring satellites take photos and send the information to Earth.

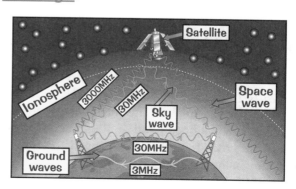

It'd be so much easier to learn if you could SEE them...

They might want you to reproduce that diagram (just above this box) to explain the difference between ground waves, sky waves and space waves. Try to remember the shape of all the wiggles too — it might remind you which waves are high frequency and which are low frequency. Worth a go anyway.

Transducers

There are Three Main Types of Transducer

They're handy little things — and there are loads of different types, as you can imagine.

TRANSDUCERS TRANSFER ENERGY FROM ONE FORM INTO ANOTHER

A Loudspeaker changes Electrical Energy into Sound Energy

You need to know about moving-coil loudspeakers — so called because they involve a coil of wire that... well, moves.

There's more on electromagnetism in the Double Science book — go there for the basics.

1) An alternating electrical signal from an amplifier passes through the wires into the coil.
2) The current in the coil turns it into an electromagnet with a North Pole and a South Pole. The direction of the current determines which pole is at which end.
3) The coil is attracted to or repelled by the permanent magnet (depending where the poles are).
4) Since the permanent magnet is fixed, the coil moves. (The larger the current, the further it moves.)
5) The coil is connected to the paper cone that moves with it.
6) As the current rapidly changes direction, so does the movement of the coil and cone. The cone vibrates, producing a sound wave of the same frequency as the alternating electrical signal. (How loud the sound is depends on how far the cone moves in and out.)

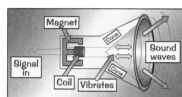

A Microphone changes Sound Energy into Electrical Energy

A microphone is like a reverse loudspeaker. There are several types of microphone — you only need to know about the moving-coil microphone:

1) Sound waves make a diaphragm vibrate.
2) The coil is attached to the diaphragm and it moves backwards and forwards past the permanent magnet.
3) This induces a current in the coil. The direction of the current depends on which way the coil is moving.

(The higher the frequency of the sound, the more rapidly the current changes direction. The louder the sound, the larger the current induced.)

4) The current signal from the microphone is amplified and then recorded or sent to a loudspeaker.

Magnetic Tape Recorders Use Magnetism — derr...

OK, so they're a few decades out of date, but you still need to know how they work. A cassette stores information on a long ribbon of tape containing iron oxide (or similar magnetic substance). In the tape machine there are 3 heads:

1) *RECORDING HEAD* — The signal from an amplifier passes into the coil, creating a strong magnetic field in the tiny gap in the tape head. As the tape passes the head, the iron oxide becomes magnetised to match the signal. As the size and frequency of the signal varies, the magnetic field varies, producing a pattern of magnetised areas on the tape.
2) *PLAYBACK HEAD* — The magnetised tape passes over the playback head and induces a small current in the coil. The current is passed to a loudspeaker after being amplified.
3) *ERASE HEAD* — The max. frequency recorded on the tape will be less than 20 kHz (the limit of our hearing). A high frequency (> 50 kHz) alternating current passes through the coil of the erase head. This removes any pattern — it demagnetises the tape.

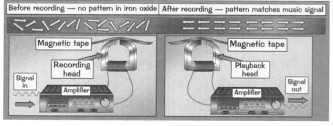

Arghhh — a three-headed monster...

Of course the down side of tapes is that they all end up mangled and get stuck in your machine. Humph.

Optical Devices

Lenses are usually made of glass or plastic. All lenses change the direction of rays of light by refraction — light slows down when it enters the lens and speeds up when it leaves.
(Look back at the Double Science book to refresh your memory about refraction.)

Converging and Diverging Lenses do Different Things

There are two main types of lens — converging and diverging.
They have different shapes and have opposite effects on light rays:

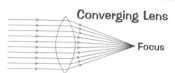

1) A converging lens is convex — it bulges outwards.
   It causes rays of light to converge (move together) to a focus.

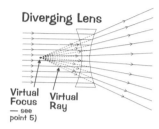

2) A diverging lens is concave — it caves inwards.
   It causes rays of light to diverge (spread out).

Learn these diagrams — you need to know all of the following:

1) the position of the focus for each lens,

2) that each ray of light changes direction when it enters and when it leaves the lens,

3) that the solid lines are called real rays as they represent where light has really travelled,

4) that the dashed lines on the diverging lens diagram are called virtual rays (as they're not really there),

5) that the virtual rays are drawn to show the point (focus) where the diverging rays appear to come from.

Taking a Photo Forms an Image on the Film

When you take a photograph of a tree, light from the object (tree) travels to the camera and is focused by the lens forming an image on the film.

1) The image on the film is a real image because light rays actually meet there.

2) The image is smaller than the object since the lens has focused the rays onto the film by refracting the light.

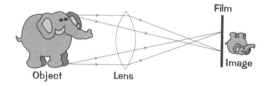

3) The image is inverted — upside down.

4) The same thing happens in our eye — a real, inverted image forms on the retina.

A Virtual Image — It's Not Really There

1) A virtual image is different from a real image.

2) A real image is where the light actually hits the screen where the image is formed — like a photo or a movie at the cinema where you see an image of the film on the giant screen.

3) When you look in a mirror you see an image of yourself behind the mirror. This is a virtual image, since light can't possibly have passed through the back of the mirror (check for yourself).

4) A similar thing happens with a converging lens used as a magnifying glass to look at a very small toy elephant.

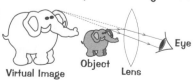

Concave lenses — come with a free cave...

Did you know... the German word for 'lens' is 'Linse' — which also means 'lentil'. Anyway...
Remember — concave caves in at the middle, convex does the opposite.

Resonance

You know that opera woman smashing glasses with her high pitched voice... well, that's what this is.

Everything has a Natural Frequency

EXAMPLES: Give a kid on a swing a push and it'll swing backwards and forwards, at a certain rate (frequency).
Gently flick the lip of a decent wine glass and it'll vibrate, 'singing' a particular note.
If a strong gust of wind hits a tall tower it'll vibrate back and forth at a certain frequency.
Everything, given a bit of energy and left to get on with it, will vibrate at its own natural frequency.

Resonance is when the Natural Frequency is Matched

EXAMPLE: When you're pushing a kid on a swing, you need to push in time with the swing to transfer the maximum energy to the kid. Otherwise it just disrupts the rhythm and the thing just wobbles about all over the place (which wastes energy).

IN GENERAL: When you force an object to vibrate, it's most effective when the driving frequency (the frequency of your 'pushes') matches the natural frequency of the object — then you get resonance.

> **RESONANCE** happens when **DRIVING FREQUENCY = NATURAL FREQUENCY**

Examples of Resonance: (other than the opera singer's broken wine glass)

1) **PENDULUM**
The kid on a swing is a simple pendulum.
The period and frequency of the pendulum depends on its length.
If you push at the natural frequency of the swing,
the amplitude of the oscillation increases rapidly.

2) **MASS ON A SPRING**

This system has a natural frequency of 2.5 Hz. A driving oscillator (a machine that makes things vibrate at a chosen frequency) makes it vibrate at a varying frequency rising from 0 to 5 Hz. At low frequencies the mass oscillates with small amplitude. As the natural frequency is reached the amplitude rises rapidly — the driver is transferring a lot of energy to the mass. Above 2.5 Hz the amplitude falls again.
(Changing the mass can change the natural frequency — increasing the mass decreases the natural frequency.)

Amplitude
of Mass
Oscillation

2.5 Hz Driving
Frequency

3) **VIBRATING STRING**
If the driving oscillator above is attached to a stretched string, a more complex effect occurs because the string has more than one resonant frequency (see next page). When the driver reaches each of these frequencies, the string vibrates in a clear pattern with large amplitude.

4) **COLUMN OF AIR IN AN OBOE**
The air inside an oboe can be made to vibrate. (It also has more than one resonant frequency).
When you blow on the reed, sound waves of many frequencies travel down the air in the oboe.
The natural frequency is 'picked out', resonance occurs and the resonant frequencies get louder
— and a musical note is heard. The natural frequency depends on the length of the column of
air. *(The longer the column the lower the natural frequency and the lower the pitch of the note.)*

5) **MICROWAVING FOOD**
Water molecules have a natural frequency matched by the frequency of microwaves.
Microwaves make the water molecules in the food resonate, transferring lots of energy to heat the food.

Natural frequency of bridge disasters — 1 every 60 years...

In 1940, the Tacoma Narrows Bridge collapsed because the wind made it resonate. "We'll never do that again," they said. 60 years later: "We've built this great Millennium Bridge over the Thames..." Hmm.

Modes of Vibration

A string has several resonant frequencies. Which means when you're playing a stringed instrument, you can get loads of groovy effects with things called 'harmonics'. It's not only true of strings, but that's all I need to tell you about for GCSE Physics. ☺

Any Multiple of the Natural Frequency will be Resonant

I'll start with the standard experiment. Set up a <u>driving oscillator</u> at one end of a <u>stretched string</u>, and <u>fix</u> the other end. <u>Waves travel</u> down the string and <u>reflect</u> off the fixed end. <u>Vary</u> the frequency of the waves, and as it approaches one of the <u>resonant frequencies</u> you get a '<u>standing wave</u>' like this:

Nodes are Stationary Points on the String

At resonant frequencies there are points where the string does not move — called '<u>nodes</u>'. The rest of the string oscillates, making pretty 'loop' <u>patterns</u> too. You can tell <u>which resonant frequency</u> the string is vibrating at by <u>counting</u> how many oscillating <u>loops</u> there are <u>between nodes</u>.

The string on the right is vibrating at the <u>fundamental frequency</u> — the <u>lowest resonant frequency</u>. <u>Half a wavelength</u> fits on the string. The only nodes here are at the <u>ends</u> of the string. There's just <u>one 'loop'</u>.

This is the <u>second harmonic</u> (or <u>first overtone</u>). It occurs at <u>twice</u> the <u>fundamental frequency</u>. <u>One whole wavelength</u> fits on the string. There is now a <u>node</u> in the <u>middle</u> and <u>ends</u>, and <u>two 'loops'</u> between.

This is the <u>third harmonic</u> (or <u>second overtone</u>). It occurs at <u>3 times</u> the <u>fundamental frequency</u>. <u>1½ wavelengths</u> fit on the string. There are now <u>four nodes</u> in total, with <u>three 'loops'</u> between them.

For Low Notes you need Long, Heavy, Loose Strings...

Guitars need to be tuned to stop them playing the wrong note (frequency). A guitar player can play a range of notes by choosing <u>different</u> strings or by <u>shortening</u> a string with their fingers. Three things can be changed to <u>alter the natural frequency</u> of a string.

1) <u>*The longer the string, the lower the note*</u>. This is because the half-wavelength you get at the natural frequency is longer. To make a higher pitched note you can shorten the string, which shortens the wavelength and increases the frequency. On a guitar you do this by pressing down on a higher fret.

   2) <u>*The heavier the string, the lower the note*</u>. Waves travel slower in a heavier string, so for any given length, a heavier string will have a lower natural frequency. You can play a higher pitched note on a guitar by plucking a lighter (thinner) string.

      3) <u>*The looser the string, the lower the note*</u>. Waves travel faster in a tighter string. For any given length a tighter string will have a higher natural frequency. You can play higher notes on a guitar by tightening the string.

Just like for low pants you need to loosen the elastic...

...though I don't recommend trying it.

Interference of Waves

Waves can interfere with each other, you know. Uh-huh. If you've got two big speakers in a big hall, you can get areas of loud and quiet bits, where the waves have either added to each other or cancelled out. Ever wanted to be a music techie? Then read this. Never wanted to be a music techie? Read it anyway.

When Waves Meet they Cause a Disturbance (just like teenagers)

1) All waves cause some kind of disturbance in a medium — water waves disturb water particles, sound waves disturb air particles, electromagnetic waves disturb electric and magnetic fields.

2) When two waves meet at a point they both try to cause their own disturbance.

3) Waves either disturb in the same direction (constructive interference), or in opposite directions (destructive interference).

4) Think of a 'pulse' travelling down a slinky spring meeting a pulse travelling in the opposite direction. These diagrams show the possible outcomes:

| | BEFORE | MEETING | AFTER |

5) The total amplitude of the waves at that point is the sum of the displacements (you have to take direction into account) of the waves at that point.

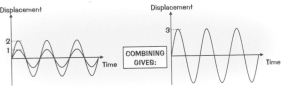

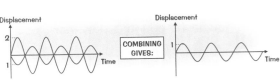

You get Patterns of 'Loud' and 'Quiet' Bits

Two speakers both play the same note, starting at exactly the same time, and are arranged as shown:

Depending on where you stand in front of them, you'll either hear a loud sound or almost nothing.

Loud	Path diff = λ
Quiet	Path difference = $\frac{\lambda}{2}$
Loud	No path difference
Quiet	Path difference = $\frac{\lambda}{2}$
Loud	Path diff = λ

1) At certain points, the sound waves will be in phase — here you get constructive interference. The amplitude of the waves will be doubled, so you'll hear a loud sound.

2) These points occur where the distance travelled by the waves from both speakers is either the same or different by a whole number of wavelengths.

3) At certain other points the sound waves will be exactly out of phase — here you get destructive interference and the waves will cancel out. This means you'll hear almost no sound.

4) These out of phase points occur where the difference in the distance travelled by the waves (the "path difference") is ½ wavelength, 1½ wavelengths, 2½ wavelengths etc.

Interference helped us Understand Light Better

1) Observing interference patterns with water waves, sound waves and microwaves is relatively easy because their wavelengths are quite large.

2) Observing interference effects with light waves is more difficult because their wavelengths are so small. Path differences with light waves have therefore got to be really tiny.

3) A chap called Young managed it by shining light through a pair of narrow slits that were just a fraction of a millimetre apart. This light then hit a screen in a dark room. There was an interference pattern of light bands (constructive) and dark bands (destructive) on the screen.

4) He was able to calculate the wavelength of light and help physicists unravel some of its mysteries...

You get to play with a slinky? — yay...

This stuff's pretty straightforward — you either add waves or take one away from the other. The sound pattern in the middle is a bit more fiddly — start by learning the diagram and it'll make more sense.

Revision Summary for Section Eight

That's all for this section, folks. Good night. Toodle pip. Missing you already.
Well, not quite...

If you reckon you know all the stuff in this section, here's how to find out for sure. Do all of these questions (don't miss any out — that's cheating). If you find any tricky, you've got more learning to do. Don't assume you know this stuff till you can comfortably answer all of these questions.

1) What is the difference between analogue and digital signals?
2) Is a vinyl record an example of analogue or digital storage?
3) Is a CD an example of analogue or digital storage?
4) How are 0s and 1s stored on a CD?
5) How are 0s and 1s read during the playback of a CD?
6) Will a CD or a vinyl record be more affected by a small scratch?
7) How are 0s and 1s sent down an optical fibre?
8) Give two advantages of sending information down an optical fibre rather than a copper wire.
9) Noise can be dealt with more easily with digital signals than with analogue. Why?
10) Draw diagrams to show how information is encoded on a carrier wave by
    a) amplitude modulation (AM), and b) frequency modulation (FM).
11) Describe the role of the capacitor in the simple demodulator in a radio.
12) Describe how the frequency of a radio wave determines whether it travels mainly as a ground wave, a sky wave or a space wave.
13) What is the difference between an active and a passive satellite?
14) What is the function of a transducer?
15) What causes the cone of a loudspeaker to vibrate?
16) What causes a current to be induced in the coil of a microphone?
17) What are the three heads that a tape recorder might have?
18) Describe how a tape recorder records information on magnetic tape.
19) What are virtual rays?
20) List three characteristics of the image that's formed when you take a photo of a building.
21) Use the example of a magnifying glass to explain the meaning of a virtual image. (Include a ray diagram.)
22) What is meant by the natural frequency of an object?
23) When does resonance occur? What happens during resonance?
24) What happens to the natural frequency of a mass on a spring if the mass is decreased?
25) Draw the pattern formed for the third harmonic on a stretched string. How many nodes are there? What happens at a node?
26) What are the three things that can be done by a cellist to play a lower note?
27) What is meant by constructive interference?
28) What is meant by destructive interference?
29) Identical sound waves leave two speakers in phase.
    At point A there is constructive interference and at point B there is destructive interference.
    Give one possible path difference at each of points A and B.
30) Why does my head hurt?

Temperature and Pressure in Gases

Absolute zero and the <u>Kelvin</u> scale of temperature — ooh, sounds like fun...

Absolute Zero *is as Cold as Stuff can get* — *0 kelvins*

1) If you <u>increase</u> the <u>temperature</u> of something, you give its particles more <u>energy</u> — they move about more <u>quickly</u> or <u>vibrate</u> a bit more. In the same way, if you <u>cool</u> a substance down, you're reducing the <u>kinetic energy</u> of the particles.

2) The <u>coldest</u> that anything can ever get is -273 °C — this temperature is known as <u>absolute zero</u>. At absolute zero, atoms have as little <u>kinetic energy</u> as it's <u>possible</u> to get.

3) Absolute zero is the start of the <u>Kelvin</u> scale of temperature.

4) A temperature change of <u>1 °C</u> is also a change of <u>1 kelvin</u>. The two scales are pretty similar — the only difference is where the <u>zero</u> occurs.

5) To convert from <u>degrees Celsius to kelvins</u>, just <u>add 273</u>. And to convert from <u>kelvins to degrees Celsius</u>, just <u>subtract 273</u>.

K	°C
283	10
273	0
263	-10
253	-20

	Absolute zero	Freezing point of water	Boiling point of water
Celsius scale	-273 °C	0 °C	100 °C
Kelvin scale	0 K	273 K	373 K

Absolute zero is actually around <u>-273.15 °C</u>, but hardly anyone bothers about the 0.15.

Kinetic Energy *is Proportional to* Temperature

The heading makes this sound more complicated than it actually is...

1) If you <u>increase</u> the temperature of a gas, you give its particles <u>more energy</u>.

2) In fact, if you <u>double</u> the temperature (measured in <u>kelvins</u>), you <u>double</u> the average <u>kinetic energy</u> of the particles.

Colliding *Gas Particles Create* Pressure

Gases consist of loads of particles shooting about <u>all over the place</u>. Remember that.

1) As gas particles move about, they <u>bang into</u> each other and whatever else happens to get in the way.

2) Even though gas particles are very light, these collisions cause a <u>force</u> on the object that gets crashed into. And if the gas is in a <u>sealed container</u>, the particles hit the container's walls — creating an <u>outward pressure</u>.

3) If the gas is <u>heated</u>, the particles move <u>faster</u>. This increase in kinetic energy means that the particles hit the walls of the container <u>harder</u>, creating even more pressure. In fact, temperature and pressure are <u>proportional</u> — if you <u>double</u> the temperature, you'll <u>double</u> the pressure as well.

4) And if you put the <u>same</u> amount of gas in a <u>bigger</u> container, the pressure will decrease, as there will be fewer collisions between the gas particles and the container's walls.

5) In fact, for a <u>fixed mass</u> of gas, this is true:

$$\frac{\text{pressure} \times \text{volume}}{\text{temperature (in K)}} = \text{constant} \implies \frac{P \times V}{T} = \text{constant}$$

This applies to so-called <u>ideal gases</u>. Ideal gases are gases that are '<u>well behaved</u>', i.e. ones that this equation works for... Scientists, eh.

Absolute zero — a common score among English cricketers...

It's weird to think that things don't get any colder than <u>zero kelvins</u> (or -273 °C). I mean, what if you had a really top-of-the-range fridge that went <u>really</u> cold... You could set it to -273 °C, put in, say, a <u>jelly</u>, and then turn the fridge down a bit more. What would happen to the jelly... it's all weird...

Particles in Atoms

The basic structure of atoms, with negative <u>electrons</u> orbiting a positive <u>nucleus</u>, was discovered by Geiger, Marsden and Rutherford in their 'gold foil and alpha particles' experiment (see the Physics book). However, it turns out that things are <u>more complicated</u> than that...

Electrons <u>and</u> Positrons <u>are</u> Fundamental Particles

1) <u>Electrons</u> are very <u>small</u> in size, <u>weigh</u> hardly anything, and are <u>negatively charged</u>.

2) Electrons are also <u>fundamental particles</u> — meaning you can't divide electrons into even <u>smaller</u> particles.

3) Electrons have a positive equivalent called <u>positrons</u>. Positrons are like electrons (they're the <u>same</u> size and mass, for example), but they're <u>positively charged</u>.

4) Positrons are also <u>fundamental</u> particles.

Protons <u>and</u> Neutrons <u>are made up of</u> Smaller Particles

1) <u>Protons</u> and <u>neutrons</u> are <u>NOT</u> <u>fundamental</u> particles. They're made up of even smaller particles called <u>quarks</u>. It takes <u>three quarks</u> to make a proton or neutron.

2) There are various kinds of quark, but protons and neutrons consist of just two types — <u>up-quarks</u> and <u>down-quarks</u>.

3) A <u>proton</u> is made of <u>two up-quarks</u> and <u>one down-quark</u>.

4) A <u>neutron</u> is made of <u>two down-quarks</u> and <u>one up-quark</u>.

5) The <u>charges</u> on up and down quarks are shown in the table. When quarks <u>combine</u> to make protons and neutrons, these charges <u>add together</u> to make the overall charges on the proton and neutron.

Quark	Charge
up	$\frac{2}{3}$
down	$-\frac{1}{3}$

Proton

'up-quark' + 'up-quark' + 'down-quark', so charge on proton $= \frac{2}{3} + \frac{2}{3} + -\frac{1}{3} = +1$

Remember: protons are 'positive'
— they're more 'up' than 'down'.

Neutron

'up-quark' + 'down-quark' + 'down-quark', so charge on neutron $= \frac{2}{3} + -\frac{1}{3} + -\frac{1}{3} = 0$

Quarks Change — producing Electrons/Positrons in the process

Sometimes the number of <u>protons</u> and <u>neutrons</u> in the nucleus can result in the atom being <u>unstable</u>. So to become more <u>stable</u>, the particles in the nucleus may change.

1) Sometimes down-quarks can <u>change</u> into up-quarks, and vice versa.

2) When this happens in a nucleus, a neutron is <u>converted</u> into a proton, or a proton into a neutron.

3) However, the <u>overall charge</u> before and after has to be <u>equal</u>. So when a <u>neutron</u> changes into a <u>proton</u>, a <u>negatively charged</u> particle also has to be produced (so that the overall charge remains <u>zero</u>).

4) The negatively charged particle produced when a neutron changes into a proton is just an <u>electron</u>. This electron is then <u>ejected</u> from the nucleus in a process called β⁻ (<u>beta minus</u>) decay. (This is just normal <u>beta radiation</u>.)

5) When a <u>proton</u> changes into a <u>neutron</u> (i.e., when an <u>up-quark</u> changes into a <u>down-quark</u>), an extra <u>positive</u> charge is needed to keep the overall charge at +1. So the nucleus produces and throws out a <u>positron</u>. This is known as β⁺ (<u>beta plus</u>) decay.

My house is like a neutron — one up, two down...

Right then... it's all getting weirder and weirder. So particles can change and become something else, can they — but only if <u>another particle</u> is produced at the same time. Hmm... it all sounds a bit <u>fishy</u> to me. Kind of like saying that a dog can change into a cat, but only if a hamster is produced as well.

Radioactive Decay

It's handy to know whether a particular nucleus is stable or unstable (since unstable ones are radioactive).
It all depends on the balance between the number of protons (Z) and the number of neutrons (N).

Big Atoms need More Neutrons than Protons to be Stable

1) The N-Z plot shows whether or not a nucleus with Z protons and N neutrons will be stable.

2) You plot the number of protons (Z) in an isotope against the number of neutrons (N) — if the point lies near the line of stability, it's stable.

3) The line of stability starts off straight, meaning that small atoms need as many neutrons as protons to be stable.

4) But for larger numbers of protons, the line curves upwards. This means that bigger atoms need more neutrons than protons to be stable.

5) If an isotope does not lie near the line, the isotope is unstable and therefore radioactive.

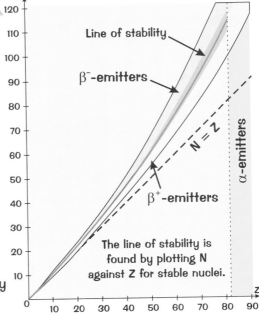

The line of stability is found by plotting N against Z for stable nuclei.

You can Predict the type of Radioactive Decay

Using the N-Z plot, you can predict what kind of radiation (if any) an isotope will give off.

1) Isotopes that have more than 82 protons in the nucleus usually try to become more stable by emitting an alpha particle.

2) Isotopes above the line of stability have too many neutrons to be stable. This means that they will undergo β⁻ decay (where a neutron is converted to a proton and an electron).

3) Isotopes beneath the line have too few neutrons. They undergo β⁺ decay (where a proton is converted to a neutron plus a positron).

4) With both β⁻ and β⁺ decay, the particles in the nucleus usually rearrange themselves, and need to get rid of an extra bit of energy as a result — this is done by emitting gamma radiation.

Nuclear Equations need to Balance

In radioactive decay, what you start with is the parent element, and what you get is the daughter element.

A typical β⁻ emission	
$^{14}_{6}C \rightarrow {}^{14}_{7}N + {}^{0}_{-1}\beta$	1) A neutron changes into an electron (which gets kicked out) plus a proton. 2) So the total number of particles in the nucleus doesn't change, i.e. the mass number (on top) stays the same. 3) But the extra proton means the atomic number goes up by one.

A typical β⁺ emission	
$^{30}_{15}P \rightarrow {}^{30}_{14}N + {}^{0}_{+1}\beta$	1) A proton changes into a positron (which gets kicked out) plus a neutron. 2) So again the total number of particles in the nucleus doesn't change, i.e. the mass number stays the same. 3) But the 'lost' proton means the atomic number goes down by one.

Always check that the mass numbers and atomic numbers in a nuclear equation balance.

The line of stability — walk along it to prove you're sober...

A bit of normality returns after the last page, which was pretty weird... That bit about balancing the mass and atomic numbers 'before' and 'after' is important. It basically means that the overall charge and the overall mass is the same before and after a radioactive decay. Which makes sense to me.

Nuclear Fission

Nuclear fission is the process used in nuclear power stations. It involves splitting a large atom into two smaller ones, which in turn releases energy.

The Splitting of Uranium-235 needs Neutrons

Uranium-235 (i.e. a uranium atom with a total of 235 protons and neutrons) is used in some nuclear reactors (and bombs).

1) Uranium-235 (U-235) is actually quite stable, so it needs to be made unstable before it'll split.

2) This is done by firing slow-moving neutrons at the U-235 atom.

3) The neutron joins the nucleus to create U-236, which is unstable.

4) The U-236 then splits into two smaller atoms, plus 2 or 3 fast-moving neutrons.

5) There are different pairs of atoms that U-236 can split into — e.g. krypton-90 and barium-144.

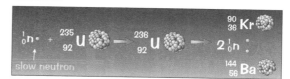

You can split More than One Atom — Chain Reactions

1) To get a useful amount of energy, loads of U-235 atoms have to be split. So neutrons released from previous fissions are used to hit other U-235 atoms.

2) These cause more atoms to (eventually) split, releasing even more neutrons, which hit even more U-235 atoms... and so on and so on. This process is known as a chain reaction.

3) However, neutrons released from the splitting of an atom move too fast to be ideal for converting U-235 into U-236. So a graphite "moderator" is used to slow down the neutrons in the reactor.

4) The fission of an atom of uranium releases loads of energy, in the form of the kinetic energy of the two new atoms (which is basically heat).

Inside a Gas-Cooled Nuclear Reactor

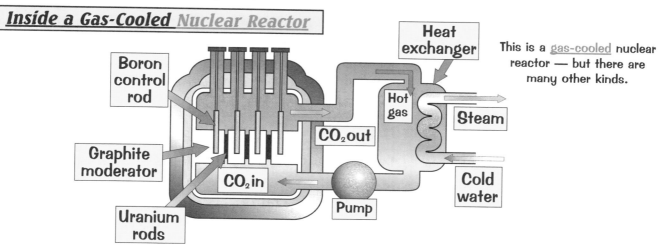

This is a gas-cooled nuclear reactor — but there are many other kinds.

1) Neutrons are injected into the reactor to "kick-start" the fission process.

2) The two fission fragments then collide with surrounding atoms, causing the temperature in the reactor to rise.

3) Control rods, often made of boron, limit the rate of fission by absorbing excess neutrons.

4) A gas, typically carbon dioxide, is pumped through the reactor in order to carry away the heat generated.

5) The gas is then passed through the heat exchanger, where it gives its energy to water — this water is heated and turned into steam, which is then used to turn the turbines, generating electricity.

Soon microchips will work this way — nuclear fission chips...

The products left over after nuclear fission are generally radioactive, so they can't just be thrown away. Sometimes they're put in thick metal containers, which are then placed in a deep hole, which is then filled with concrete. But some people worry that the materials could leak out after a number of years. Hmm.

Electron Guns

Electron guns are what you have in your telly. They fire electrons at the screen.

Electron Guns _use_ Thermionic Emission

1) The heater passes energy to the electrons in the cathode. Once they have enough energy, they "boil off", i.e. they escape. This process is called thermionic emission.

2) The electrons then accelerate as they're pulled towards the (positive) anode.

3) An electric field created between two charged metal plates can be used to deflect the electrons. Using two pairs of plates (the X- and Y-plates), the electron beam can be deflected both up and down (by the Y-plates) and left and right (by the X-plates).

4) In things like television tubes, computer monitors and oscilloscopes, the electrons hit a screen covered in chemicals like phosphorus. These chemicals emit light when hit by electrons.

5) But electron beams can also be used to produce X-rays. When the electrons hit a tungsten target, their kinetic energy is converted into X-rays.

Diagram labels: 3 kV, Heater, -ve, +ve, Phosphorescent screen, Electrons attracted towards anode, Cathode, Electrons emitted from cathode, Glass tube containing vacuum, Anode, Deflecting plates

One Equation that's Bound to be in the Exam

1) The kinetic energy gained by the electrons is given by:

kinetic energy = charge of the electron (q) × accelerating voltage (V)

$$\frac{KE}{q \times V}$$

2) The beam of electrons produced is equivalent to an electrical current. This means the beam must follow the rules and formulas that are linked to currents, e.g. charge (Q) = current (I) × time (t)

Oscilloscopes are used to Test Electrical Signals

An oscilloscope is a device for checking the voltage and frequency of an electrical signal.

1) The screen is divided by equally spaced lines that are used in the same way as gridlines on a graph.

2) The horizontal (x) axis represents time, and the vertical (y) axis represents voltage.

3) The electron beam is made to move in the x-direction by the X-plates. How quickly the beam moves across the screen is set using the timebase control, which controls the amount of time per division.

4) The vertical (y) axis is set using the volts per division control (which controls the Y-plates). You adjust that according to the electrical signal you're testing.

Time for 1 wave = 40 ms = 0.04 s
Frequency is number of waves per second
= 1 ÷ 0.04 = 25 Hz

Maximum voltage = 4 V

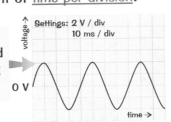

Settings: 2 V / div, 10 ms / div

Electron guns — it all sounds a bit Star Trek to me...

There's a lot on this page about electron guns. But to be sure you'll be able to answer any question on the subject come Exam time, you need to make sure you know all the normal electricity equations from the Double Science Physics book as well. They're all there — so take the time to learn them...

Revision Summary for Section Nine

Some of this stuff can be just learnt and regurgitated — other parts actually need thinking about. It's made even harder by the fact that you can't see any of it happening in everyday life. You just have to take my word for it — it happens. If you can answer these questions, you should have no problem with almost anything the Examiners throw at you. But if any of these questions stump you, go back and learn the stuff — then give it another go.

1) What temperature is absolute zero in °C?

2) What is the boiling point of water in kelvins?

3) Convert 25 °C into kelvins.

4) What happens to the average kinetic energy of gas molecules when the temperature changes from 100 K to 300 K?

5) Describe what happens to the pressure of a gas in a sealed container when the temperature is reduced.

6) Can a positron be split into any smaller particles?

7) What three particles make up a proton?

8) What charge does an up-quark have?

9) Describe the changes of quark that happen when beta decay occurs.

10) Write out the nuclear equation for the beta decay of carbon-14.

11) If a lightweight isotope is plotted on the N-Z stability curve and appears underneath the line of stability, what type of decay is it likely to undergo?

12) How is an atom with 98 protons likely to decay?

13) How do atoms get rid of excess energy after beta decay?

14) What type of particle is U-235 bombarded with to make it split?

15) What is used in a reactor to slow down neutrons which are moving too quickly?

16) Describe how nuclear fission can be used to generate electricity.

17) Explain the problems of storing waste products from the nuclear fission process.

18) What term is used to describe how electrons are emitted from the cathode in an electron gun?

19) How can a beam of charged particles in an electron gun be deflected?

20) What is the purpose of having a phosphorescent screen at the end of an oscilloscope tube?

21) Calculate the amount of kinetic energy gained by an electron (charge on an electron = -1.6×10^{-19} C) when it is accelerated through a voltage of:
   - a) 10 V
   - b) 1000 V
   - c) 5 kV

22) What is the current of a beam of electrons when 0.002 C of charge hit the screen every second?

23) What is represented by the y-axis of an oscilloscope screen?

24) Draw diagrams to show what you would see on an oscilloscope if these signals were put in:
   - a) an alternating signal with time period 20 ms and a peak voltage of 2 V
   - b) an alternating signal with frequency 50 Hz and a peak voltage of 230 V

Electronic Systems

There are three main parts of an electronic system. And you need to know everything about all three parts — but that's fine, as they're pretty easy to get your head round really.

Electronic Systems = Input, Process, Output

| Input Sensor | → | Processor | → | Output Device |

1) **Input sensors** (e.g. thermistors and LDRs) — these detect changes in the surroundings, such as changes in temperature, light, magnetic field, moisture or movement, and then send signals to...

2) **Processors** (e.g. logic gates and transistors) — these 'examine' the inputs and 'decide' what response is needed — they then send a 'message' to...

3) **Output devices** (e.g. bulbs and buzzers) — these produce light, sound, movement, heat, etc.

A Relay is a Posh Switch
The internal workings of a relay are in the Physics book.

1) A relay connects two circuits. It's basically a switch that turns the second circuit on when a current flows through the first circuit.

2) The output of an electronic system can allow a small current to flow through the relay in the first circuit. The relay then switches on a larger current in the second circuit that contains an output device like a motor.

3) A relay is needed in electronics for two reasons:

   i) The output of the electronic system (e.g. logic gate) can't supply enough power or current to work output devices like motors and heaters.

   ii) It isolates the low voltage electronic system (that a person might come into contact with, e.g. in a car) from the high voltage mains often needed for the output device (e.g. the car's starter motor).

This is the circuit symbol for a relay.

A Transistor is a Really Posh Switch

1) A transistor is a complicated device (usually about the size of a raisin), but a computer chip contains thousands of microscopic ones.

2) The most important thing to know is that they can act as switches.

3) A transistor has 3 connections. Once the voltage at the base is high enough, the transistor 'switches on' and allows a current to flow from the collector to the emitter.

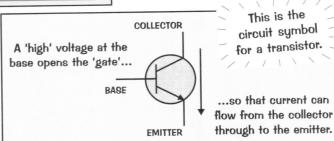

This is the circuit symbol for a transistor.

A 'high' voltage at the base opens the 'gate'... ...so that current can flow from the collector through to the emitter.

COLLECTOR

BASE

EMITTER

Learn these Extra Circuit Symbols

As well as the circuit symbols in the Physics book, you need to know these ones here...

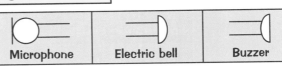

Microphone   Electric bell   Buzzer

If I were you, I wouldn't relay on last-minute revision...

Transistors and relays — they sound pretty complicated, but knowing that they're essentially switches helps to demystify them a bit. There are three sections on this page (plus a few circuit symbols) — cover the page and do a mini-essay for each section to see how well you know it all.

Logic Gates

Learning about <u>logic gates</u> was probably how Bill Gates (no pun intended) got started. So learn all this stuff, then design a computer operating system that crashes a lot... Bob's your uncle.

Digital Systems are either On or Off

1) Every connection in a digital system is in one of only <u>two states</u>. They can be either ON or OFF, either HIGH or LOW, either YES or NO, either 1 or 0... you get the picture.

2) In reality a 1 is a <u>high voltage</u> (about 5 V) and a 0 is a <u>low voltage</u> (about 0 V). Any part of the system is in one of these two states — nothing in between.

3) The state of an output can be shown <u>visually</u> by connecting an LED (with a protective resistor) as shown.

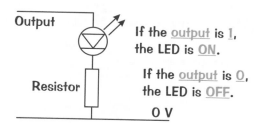

If the <u>output</u> is <u>1</u>, the LED is <u>ON</u>.

If the <u>output</u> is <u>0</u>, the LED is <u>OFF</u>.

Logic Gates are a type of Digital Processor

<u>Logic gates</u> are small, but they're made up of <u>lots</u> of really small components like <u>transistors</u> and <u>resistors</u>.

Each type of logic gate has its own set of <u>rules</u> for converting inputs to outputs, and these rules are best shown in <u>truth tables</u>. The important thing is to list <u>all</u> the possible <u>combinations</u> of input values.

NOT gate — sometimes called an Inverter

A <u>NOT</u> gate just has <u>one</u> input — and this input can be either <u>1</u> or <u>0</u>, so the truth table has just two rows.

Input	Output
0	1
1	0

AND and OR gates usually have Two Inputs

Some AND and OR gates have more than two inputs, but you don't have to worry about those.

<u>Each input</u> can be 0 or 1, so to allow for <u>all</u> combinations from two inputs, your truth table needs <u>4 rows</u>.

There's a certain logic to the names — e.g. an <u>AND</u> gate only gives an output of 1 if both the first input <u>AND</u> the second input are 1. An <u>OR</u> gate just needs either the first <u>OR</u> the second input to be 1.

Input A	Input B	Output
0	0	0
1	0	0
0	1	0
1	1	1

Input A	Input B	Output
0	0	0
1	0	1
0	1	1
1	1	1

You'll quite often see an OR gate drawn like this:

NAND and NOR gates have the Opposite Output of AND and OR gates

A <u>NAND</u> gate gives the <u>opposite</u> output to a normal AND gate — e.g. if an AND gate would give an output of 0, a <u>NAND</u> gate would give 1, and vice versa.

Input A	Input B	Output
0	0	1
1	0	1
0	1	1
1	1	0

Input A	Input B	Output
0	0	1
1	0	0
0	1	0
1	1	0

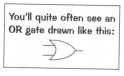

What's so hard about truth and logic...

You probably didn't realise when you rejected GCSE Philosophy and opted for Physics instead that you'd be covering the topics of <u>logic</u> and <u>truth</u> anyway. Yep, it's surprising how much the two subjects have in common. Anyway, learn all this stuff and you'll be fine come the truth section of <u>either</u> subject.

Using Logic Gates

You need to be able to construct a truth table for a combination of logic gates.
Approach this kind of thing in an organised way and stick to the rules, and you won't go far wrong.

'Interesting' Example — a Greenhouse

Check out the following example — a warning system for a greenhouse.
The gardener wants to be warned if it gets too cold or if someone has opened the door.

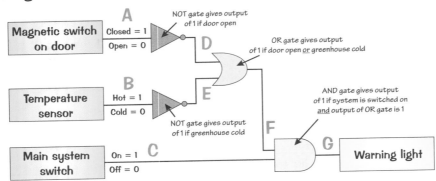

Inputs						Output
A	B	C	D	E	F	G
0	0	0	1	1	1	0
0	0	1	1	1	1	1
0	1	0	1	0	1	0
0	1	1	1	0	1	1
1	0	0	0	1	1	0
1	0	1	0	1	1	1
1	1	0	0	0	0	0
1	1	1	0	0	0	0

The warning light will come on if: (i) it is cold in the greenhouse OR if the door is opened,
(ii) AND the system is switched on.

1) Each connection has a label, and all possible combinations of the inputs are included in the table.
2) What really matters are the inputs and the output — the rest of the truth table is just there to help.

A Latch works like a kind of Memory (but is really hard to understand)

1) It's likely that the greenhouse will be too cold in the middle of the night but warm up again by morning. This means the warning light will have gone out by the time the gardener gets out of bed.

2) What the gardener needs is some way of getting the warning light to stay on until it is seen and reset. This is where the latch comes in.

3) A latch can be made by combining two NOR gates as shown. In the above system, the latch would be between the blue OR gate and the green AND gate.

(1) When the gardener goes to bed:
    Input F is 0... and output T is 0...
    ...meaning that the top NOR gate outputs 1...
    ...and so the bottom NOR gate outputs 0,
        which means... output T remains 0.

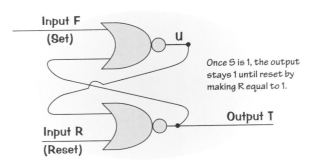

Once S is 1, the output stays 1 until reset by making R equal to 1.

(2) When the door is opened or the temperature falls:
    Input F becomes 1...
    ...so output U becomes 0...
    ...so the bottom NOR gate gives 1
        (as input R is still 0)... i.e. the output is 1.

(3) When the door is closed / the temperature rises:
    Input F becomes 0 again...
    ...but output T is 1 still...
    ...so output U stays 0 ...and output T stays 1.

(4) To reset the system:
    Briefly make input R equal to 1...
    ...and since output U is still 0...
    ...output T becomes 0.

Σιγα, σιγα*... (as they say in Greece)... *Slowly, slowly

My advice to you when you're doing questions on this stuff is don't rush. Draw a truth table, listing all the inputs and outputs, and fill it in ultra-carefully, one bit at a time.

Potential Dividers

Potential dividers consist of a pair of resistors. One of them usually has a fixed resistance, and the other's resistance varies with temperature, light intensity or something.

The Higher the Resistance, the Greater the Voltage Drop

A voltage across a pair of resistors is 'shared out' according to their relative resistances. The rule is:

The larger the share of the total resistance, the larger the share of the total voltage.

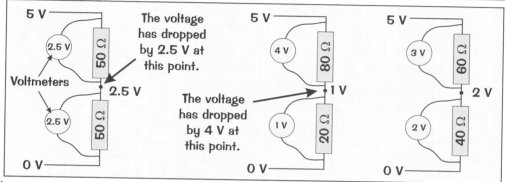

The resistances are equal, so each resistor takes half the voltage.

The top resistor has 80% of the total resistance, and so takes 80% of the total voltage.

The top resistor has 60% of the total resistance, and so takes 60% of the total voltage.

Potential Dividers are quite Useful

Potential dividers are not only spectacularly interesting — they're useful as well. But first there's an equation you need to get your head round. Rats.

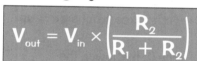

$$V_{out} = V_{in} \times \left(\frac{R_2}{R_1 + R_2} \right)$$

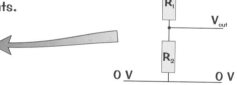

1) Using a thermistor and a variable resistor in a potential divider, you can make a temperature sensor that triggers an output device at a temperature you choose.

2) The sensor on page 79 gave an output of 1 when it was hot and an output of 0 when it was cold (the output is the point between the two resistors). This is how it works...

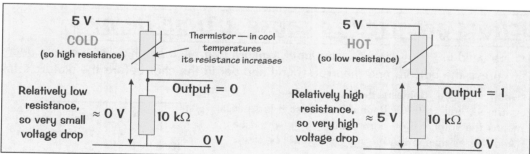

1️⃣ When the thermistor's cold its resistance is very high, so the voltage drop across it is almost 5 V, meaning the voltage of the output is nearly 0 V — a 'logical 0'.

2️⃣ As the temperature of the thermistor increases, its resistance falls dramatically. So the voltage across it is almost 0 V and the voltage of the output is nearly 5 V — a 'logical 1'.

My girlfriend's bad breath and BO is a potential divider...

You can play about with the circuit and make other kinds of sensors too. I mean, if you swap the resistor and the thermistor around in the last diagram above, you get a 'cold' sensor that gives a 1 when it's cold and a 0 when it's hot. It's all clever stuff. And kind of interesting as well. Kind of, I said.

Capacitors

A capacitor is a device that stores charge. The bigger the capacitance of a capacitor, the more charge it can store.

The More Charge Stored, the Greater the Voltage Drop

1) You charge a capacitor by connecting it to a source of voltage, e.g. a battery.

2) A current flows around the circuit, and charge gets stored on the capacitor.

3) The more charge that's stored on a capacitor, the larger the potential difference (or voltage) across it.

4) When the voltage across the capacitor is equal to that of the battery, the current stops and the capacitor is fully charged.

5) The voltage across the capacitor won't rise above the voltage of the battery.

6) If the battery is removed, the capacitor discharges.

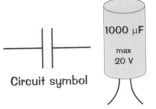

Circuit symbol

1000 μF max 20 V

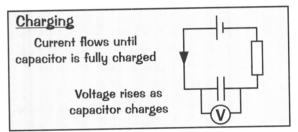

Charging

Current flows until capacitor is fully charged

Voltage rises as capacitor charges

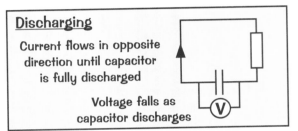

Discharging

Current flows in opposite direction until capacitor is fully discharged

Voltage falls as capacitor discharges

The Charging Time depends on the Capacitor and the Circuit

It's possible to control how long it takes for a capacitor to become fully charged (or discharged). There are two important factors — the capacitance of the capacitor and the resistance in the circuit:

1) The greater the capacitance, the more charge it takes to charge it up and so the longer it will take.

2) The larger the resistance of the charging circuit, the lower the current that flows and so the longer it will take to charge up the capacitor (remember — charge = current × time).

3) The rules for capacitor discharge are the same. The larger the capacitance and the resistance, the longer it will take.

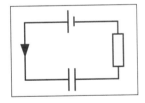

Capacitors are used to cause a Time Delay

Capacitors are used in timing circuits, and input sensors that need a delay. Like on a camera when you want to press the button, and then run round and get in the shot before the picture's taken.

1) The switch is closed. Initially, the capacitor has no charge stored, and so the voltage drop across it is small. This means the voltage drop across the resistor must be big. (And this all means the output voltage will be low).

2) As the capacitor charges, the voltage drop across it increases (and so the voltage drop across the resistor falls). This all means the voltage at the output increases.

3) The shutter on the camera will open (i.e. the picture will be taken) when the input is close to 5 V.

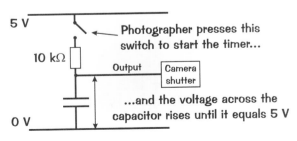

5 V

10 kΩ

Output

Photographer presses this switch to start the timer...

Camera shutter

...and the voltage across the capacitor rises until it equals 5 V

0 V

I have a low capacitance memory — I can't store much info...

The good thing about this subject is that you can see an actual use for most of the things on the page. It's all easy-to-find-a-use-for information. But that probably isn't all that surprising — this is electronics we're talking here, not alchemy. No, the GCSE Alchemy revision guide is a totally different book.

Electronic Systems in Practice

Put the stuff on the last few pages together and what do you get... well, this circuit.
And it's an examiners' favourite. So do yourself a favour — learn it well.

Examiners Love this Circuit...

It's a beauty — it acts as a light sensor that turns on a floodlight when it gets dark.

When it gets dark...

① ...the resistance of the LDR becomes high, and so the voltage drop across it increases...

② ...so the voltage here becomes close to 0 V (a logical 0)...

③ ...which is converted to a logical 1.

④ The high input into the transistor...

⑤ ...allows current to flow through the relay...

⑥ ...which switches on the current in the high-current circuit...

⑦ ...which turns on the output device (here, a floodlight).

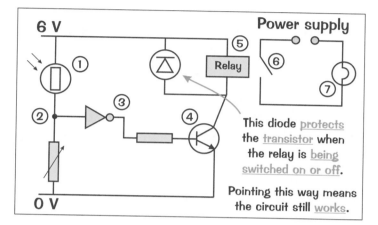

This diode protects the transistor when the relay is being switched on or off.

Pointing this way means the circuit still works.

...so make sure you know the Effects of making Changes

Exam questions often ask how the circuit above can be changed, or what the effect of a change might be.

1) The variable resistor can be used to adjust the light level that will trigger the circuit. If its resistance is increased, the light level will have to drop more before the floodlight is switched on.

2) The output device could be anything — a light, a buzzer, a motor, a heater, a lock, etc.

3) If the variable resistor and the LDR are swapped around, then the system will switch on the output device when the light intensity is high.

4) If the LDR is replaced with a thermistor, then the output device will be switched on when it gets cold.

Electronics are Everywhere... everywhere, I tell you

You'd have to be living in a cave not to be aware of the importance of electronic systems in the world...

1) In modern cars there's an array of sensors to improve safety and efficiency — e.g. sensors to prevent skidding when braking, sensors to detect a crash and set off air bags, and sensors to monitor the engine temperature and adjust fuel injection.

2) Mobile phones are dead popular nowadays — but there may be health hazards from the radiation given off by the handsets and the masts. And in theory, you can be tracked by using the signal from your mobile — a potential invasion of privacy... But unless you're on the top of a mountain, a CCTV camera has probably spotted you anyway, of course.

Ever get the feeling you're being watched...

3) The Internet has been at the centre of an information revolution — you can find out about anything by pressing a few buttons. It's provided new ways of learning (and, of course, cheating on coursework). However it does have the drawback of allowing unsuitable material to be viewed by children. (And I could go on and on about computers, videos, CDs, and so on... but I won't — use your imagination.)

I told you I wasn't being paranoid — I really was being watched...

I know what you're thinking — that circuit at the top of the page looks a bit hefty.
But if you can get your head round that, whatever they give you in the Exam won't seem too bad.

Revision Summary for Section Ten

Well gosh darn... that was only a short section, but I wouldn't be surprised if you're feeling a bit numb after going through all that. It's really hard stuff, there's no doubt about that, but just think how smug and self-satisfied you'll feel when you get your head round it. And you know what's going to help you get your head round it... yep, practice. And when you've finished practising, get some more practice. That's what I recommend, and that's where these questions come in. Try your hand at them, then check to see if you got any wrong. And if you did, I recommend some more practice.

1) Name two types of input sensor. What change in the surroundings does each type respond to?

2) What is the job of a processor in an electronic system?

3) Describe what a relay does. Give two reasons why they are used.

4) What happens when the voltage at the base of a transistor is high enough?

5) Draw the circuit symbols for a) a microphone, b) an electric bell, c) a buzzer.

6) Draw the symbol and the truth table for a) an **OR** gate, b) an **AND** gate.

7) Draw the symbol for a **NOT** gate. What does a **NOT** gate do?

8) Draw the symbol and the truth table for a **NAND** gate.

9) When will a **NOR** gate give an output of 1?

10) Copy and complete the truth table for the logic gate combination.

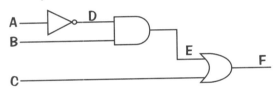

Inputs					Output
A	B	C	D	E	F
0	0	0			
0	0	1			
0	1	0			
0	1	1			
1	0	0			
1	0	1			
1	1	0			
1	1	1			

11) What is a latch used for in an electronic system?

12) Draw a latch made from two **NOR** gates.

13) For the potential divider on the right calculate:
    a) the voltage across the 50 Ω resistor
    b) the voltage across the 200 Ω resistor
    c) the voltage at the point P.

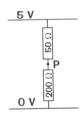

14) Look at the potential divider on the right.
    What will happen to the voltage at point **X** when a bright
    light shines on the LDR? Explain your answer.

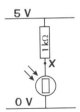

15) What happens to the potential difference (voltage) across a capacitor when more charge is stored on it?

16) In order to increase the time taken to charge a capacitor fully what should you do to:
    a) the capacitance of the capacitor
    b) the resistance of the charging circuit?

17) Give one advantage and one disadvantage of:
    a) the increased use of CCTV cameras
    b) the development of mobile phone technology
    c) the Internet.

Stretching Things

When you pull on things, they stretch. When you let go, some things go back to how they were before, and some things don't. Yep, that pretty much sums this page up.

Stretching a Steel Spring — Elastic then Plastic

The greater the stretching force on a spring, the greater the extension (i.e. the longer it gets).

① To begin with, the extension is proportional to the force — twice the force means twice the extension. And when you remove the force, the spring goes back to its original length. This is elastic behaviour.

② Once the elastic limit's reached, the spring's behaviour changes.

③ The extension isn't proportional to the force, and the spring won't go back to it's original length. This is plastic behaviour.

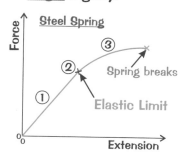

The Spring Constant only applies in the Elastic Region

The spring constant (k) is a measure of "how stiff" the spring is, i.e. how much force it takes to stretch it.

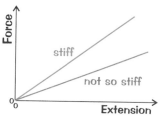

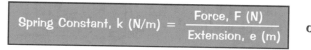

$$\text{Spring Constant, } k \text{ (N/m)} = \frac{\text{Force, F (N)}}{\text{Extension, e (m)}} \quad \text{or} \quad F = ke$$

1) The spring constant is the gradient of the "force vs extension" graph.

2) The steeper the graph, the larger the spring constant, and the stiffer the spring.

Energy Stored is the Area Under the Graph

1) The more force used to stretch a spring and the further it stretches, the more energy that's stored.

2) The area under the force/extension graph gives the energy stored in the spring.

3) This ONLY WORKS FOR ELASTIC BEHAVIOUR, though, so the area's always a triangle and you can use this formula:

$$\text{Energy Stored (J)} = \tfrac{1}{2} \text{ Force (N)} \times \text{Extension (m)}$$

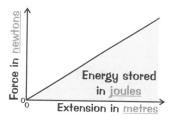

Different Things Behave Differently When Stretched

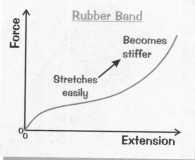

1) Rubber bands stretch easily at first — but their extension is not proportional to the force applied.

2) As the force increases, they become stiffer.

1) Copper wire stretches elastically at first.

2) After the elastic limit, the wire will be permanently stretched.

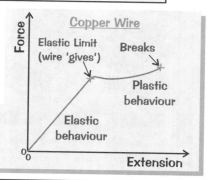

This page is meant to stretch you...

I bet you can feel your brain cells aching with all this new information. Learn each of the graphs and then cover them up and try to draw them from memory, marking all the features. And make sure you know how to use the graphs to work out the spring constant and the energy stored.

Centre of Mass and Stability

Density and centres of mass — what could be more fun...
And it's all pretty important stuff — toppling over is not a great idea for stuff like buses and buildings.

Density means How Much Mass there is in a Certain Volume

$$\text{Density } (\rho) \text{ (kg/m}^3) = \frac{\text{Mass (kg)}}{\text{Volume (m}^3)}$$

Greek letter 'rho'.

Lead is denser than foam, so 1 m³ of lead weighs more than 1 m³ of foam. And 1 tonne of lead takes up less space than 1 tonne of foam.

The Centre of Mass hangs Directly Below the Point of Suspension

1) You can think of the centre of mass of an object as the point at which the whole mass is concentrated.

2) A freely suspended object will swing until its centre of mass is vertically below the point of suspension.

3) This means you can find the centre of mass of any flat shape like this:

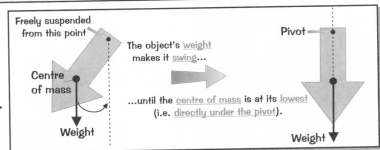

Freely suspended from this point

Centre of mass

Weight

The object's weight makes it swing...

...until the centre of mass is at its lowest (i.e. directly under the pivot).

Pivot

Weight

1) Suspend the shape and a plumb line from the same point, and wait until they stop moving.
2) Draw a line along the plumb line.
3) Do the same thing again, but suspend the shape from a different pivot point.
4) The centre of mass is where your two lines cross.

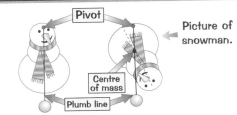

Pivot

Picture of snowman.

Centre of mass

Plumb line

4) But you don't need to go to all that trouble for simple shapes. You can quickly guess where the centre of mass is by looking for lines of symmetry.

   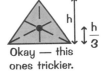

h

h/3

Okay — this ones trickier.

Low and Wide Objects are Most Stable

Unstable objects tip over easily — stable ones don't. The position of the centre of mass is all-important.

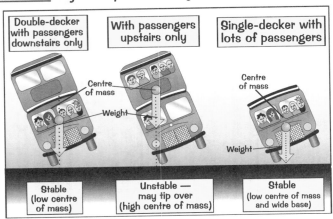

Double-decker with passengers downstairs only

With passengers upstairs only

Single-decker with lots of passengers

Centre of mass

Weight

Centre of mass

Weight

Stable (low centre of mass)

Unstable — may tip over (high centre of mass)

Stable (low centre of mass and wide base)

1) The most stable objects have a wide base and a low centre of mass.

2) An object will begin to tip over if its centre of mass moves beyond the edge of its base.

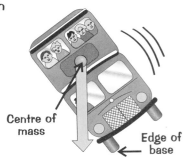

Centre of mass

Edge of base

Be the centre of mass — sit on the middle pew...

Make sure you know the equation for density as well as you know your own name. You'll feel pretty dense in the exam if you miss out on those easy marks (ho, ho, ho). You also need to be able to describe how to find the centre of mass of any shape. Shut the book and write out the method step by step.

Moments

If you've ever wondered why nuts* come undone much more easily with long spanners, you're about to find out. If you've never wondered — well, you still need to know. *You know which nuts I mean. Let's not get silly.

A Moment is the Turning Effect of a Force

MOMENT (Nm) = FORCE (N) × perpendicular DISTANCE (m) between line of action and pivot

1) The force on the spanner causes a turning effect or moment on the nut. A larger force would mean a larger moment.

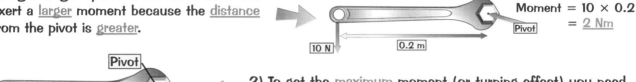

Tough nut

Force = 10 N   Distance = 0.1 m

Moment = 10 × 0.1 = 1 Nm

2) Using a longer spanner, the same force can exert a larger moment because the distance from the pivot is greater.

Pivot

10 N   0.2 m

Moment = 10 × 0.2 = 2 Nm

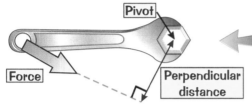

Pivot

Force   Perpendicular distance

3) To get the maximum moment (or turning effect) you need to push at right angles (perpendicular) to the spanner.

4) Pushing at any other angle means a smaller moment because the perpendicular distance between the line of action and the pivot is smaller.

A Question of Balance — Are the Moments Equal?

If the anticlockwise moments are equal to the clockwise moments, the object won't turn.

Example 1: Your younger brother weighs 300 N and sits 2 m from the pivot of a seesaw. If you weigh 700 N, where should you sit to balance the seesaw?

For the seesaw to balance:

Total Anticlockwise Moments = Total Clockwise Moments

2 m   y

300 N   700 N

anticlockwise moment = clockwise moment
$$300 \times 2 = 700 \times y$$
$$y = 0.86 \text{ m}$$

Ignore the weight of the seesaw — its centre of mass is on the pivot and doesn't have any turning effect.

Example 2: A 6 m long steel girder weighing 1000 N rests horizontally on a pole 1 m from one end. What is the tension in a supporting cable attached vertically to the other end?

The 'tension in the cable' thing makes this sound harder than it actually is. But it's balanced, so...

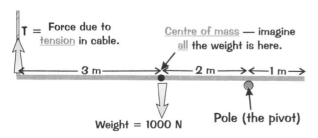

T = Force due to tension in cable.

Centre of mass — imagine all the weight is here.

3 m   2 m   1 m

Weight = 1000 N   Pole (the pivot)

anticlockwise moment (due to weight) = clockwise moment (due to tension in cable)

$$1000 \times 2 = T \times 5$$
$$2000 = 5T$$
and so $T = 400$ N

Take a moment or two to learn this page...

Seesaws. Remember the days when you were young and carefree. Now it's just revision, revision and more revision. Sigh... Ah well, let's get this over with then. The main thing to remember is that the clockwise moments must be equal to the anticlockwise moments for something to balance.

Momentum and Collisions

A <u>large</u> rugby player running very <u>fast</u> is going to be a lot harder to stop than
a scrawny one out for a Sunday afternoon stroll — that's momentum for you.

<u>Momentum = Mass × Velocity</u>

1) The <u>greater</u> the <u>mass</u> of an object and the <u>greater</u> its <u>velocity</u>,
the <u>more momentum</u> the object has.

2) Momentum is a <u>vector</u> quantity — it has size <u>and</u> direction
(like <u>velocity</u>, but not speed).

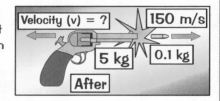

Momentum (kg m/s) = Mass (kg) × Velocity (m/s)

<u>Momentum Before</u> = <u>Momentum After</u>

<u>Momentum is conserved</u> when no forces act, i.e. the total momentum <u>after</u> is the <u>same</u> as it was <u>before</u>.

Example 1:

Two skaters approach each other, collide and move off together as shown. At what velocity do they move after the collision?

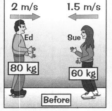

1) Choose which direction is <u>positive</u>.
I'll say "<u>positive</u>" means "<u>to the right</u>".

2) <u>Total momentum before</u> collision
= momentum of Ed + momentum of Sue
= {80 × 2} + {60 × (–1.5)} = <u>70 kg m/s</u>

3) <u>Total momentum after</u> collision
= momentum of Ed and Sue together
= <u>140 × v</u>

4) So 140v = 70, i.e. <u>v = 0.5 m/s to the right</u>

Example 2:

A gun fires a bullet as shown. At what speed does the gun move backwards?

1) Choose which direction is <u>positive</u>.
Again, I reckon "<u>positive</u>" means "<u>to the right</u>".

2) <u>Total momentum before</u> firing
= <u>0 kg m/s</u>

3) <u>Total momentum after</u> firing
= momentum of bullet + momentum of gun
= (0.1 × 150) + (5 × v)
= <u>15 + 5v</u>

This is the gun's <u>recoil</u>.

4) So 15 + 5v = 0, i.e. v = -3 m/s
So the gun moves backwards at <u>3 m/s</u>.

<u>Rockets</u> work in much the same way — they chuck a load of <u>exhaust gases</u>
out <u>backwards</u>, and since momentum is conserved, the rocket moves <u>forwards</u>.

<u>Forces Cause Changes in Momentum</u>

1) When a <u>force</u> acts on an object, it causes a <u>change</u> in momentum.

$$\text{Force acting (N)} = \frac{\text{Change in Momentum (kg m/s)}}{\text{Time taken for change to happen (s)}}$$

2) A <u>larger</u> force means a <u>faster</u> change of momentum (and so a greater <u>acceleration</u>).

3) Likewise, if someone's momentum changes <u>very quickly</u> (like in a <u>car crash</u>), the <u>forces</u> on the body will be very <u>large</u> (and more likely to cause <u>injury</u>).

4) This is why cars are designed to slow people down over a <u>longer time</u> when they have a crash — the longer it takes for a change in <u>momentum</u>, the <u>smaller</u> the <u>force</u>.

<u>CRUMPLE ZONES</u> crumple on impact, <u>increasing the time</u> taken for the car to stop.

<u>SEAT BELTS</u> stretch slightly, <u>increasing the time</u> taken for the wearer to stop. This <u>reduces the forces</u> acting on the chest.

<u>AIR BAGS</u> also slow you down more <u>slowly</u>.

<u>Momentum — that's what you need to learn this stuff...</u>

Now then... <u>momentum</u> is always <u>conserved</u> in collisions and explosions (when no other forces act),
but <u>kinetic energy</u> might not be — in fact, the kinetic energy is usually <u>a bit less</u> after a collision.
This is because most collisions are <u>inelastic</u>. (If the energy <u>is</u> conserved, it's called an <u>elastic collision</u>.)

Equations of Motion

These <u>equations of motion</u> are dead handy for working out <u>velocity</u>, <u>acceleration</u> and other goodies...

You need to know these Four Equations of Motion

Which of these equations you need to use depends on what you <u>already know</u>, and what you need to <u>find out</u>. But that means you have to know all 4 equations — preferably like the back of your hand.

Altogether, there are 5 things involved in these equations:

<u>u</u> = <u>initial velocity</u>, <u>v</u> = <u>final velocity</u>, <u>s</u> = <u>distance</u>, <u>t</u> = <u>time</u>, <u>a</u> = <u>acceleration</u>.

(1) $s = \dfrac{(u + v)t}{2}$ (2) $v = u + at$ (3) $s = ut + \dfrac{1}{2}at^2$ (4) $v^2 = u^2 + 2as$

If you know <u>three things</u>, you can find out <u>either</u> of the <u>other two</u> — if you use the <u>right equation</u>, that is. And if you use this method <u>twice</u>, you can find out <u>both</u> things you don't know.

HOW TO CHOOSE YOUR EQUATION:
1) Write down which <u>three</u> things you <u>already know</u>.
2) Write down which of the other things you want to <u>find out</u>.
3) <u>Choose</u> the equation that involves <u>all</u> of the things you've <u>written down</u>.
4) <u>Stick in</u> your numbers, and do the <u>maths</u>.

<u>Direction</u> is important for <u>velocity</u>, <u>acceleration</u> and <u>distance</u> — so always choose which direction is <u>positive</u>, and <u>stick</u> with it.

Example: *A car going at 10 m/s accelerates at 2 m/s² for 8 s. How far does the car go while accelerating?*

Now then, first things first... I'll say that the "<u>positive</u>" direction is "<u>to the right</u>".

1) You <u>already</u> know <u>u</u> (= 10 m/s), <u>a</u> (= 2 m/s²) and <u>t</u> (= 8 s).
2) You want to <u>find out s</u>.
3) So you need the equation with <u>all</u> these in: <u>u</u>, <u>a</u>, <u>t</u> and <u>s</u> — that's number 3: $s = ut + \dfrac{1}{2}at^2$.
4) Now just bung in the numbers: $s = (10 \times 8) + \dfrac{1}{2}(2 \times 8^2) = 80 + 64 = \underline{144\text{ m}}$

Projectiles — Deal with Horizontal and Vertical Motion Separately

This is very exciting now — things flying through the air, where the only force acting on them is <u>gravity</u>...

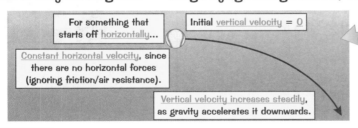

For something that starts off <u>horizontally</u>...

Initial <u>vertical velocity</u> = <u>0</u>

<u>Constant horizontal velocity</u>, since there are no horizontal forces (ignoring friction/air resistance).

<u>Vertical velocity increases steadily</u>, as gravity accelerates it downwards.

1) Motion can be split into <u>two</u> separate bits — the <u>horizontal</u> bit and the <u>vertical</u> bit.
2) These bits are totally <u>separate</u> — one doesn't affect the other.
3) So gravity (which only acts downwards) doesn't affect horizontal motion at all.

Example: *A football's kicked horizontally from a 20 m high wall. How long is it before it lands? Take g = 10 m/s².*

It lands when it's travelled 20 m vertically.
Using $s = ut + \dfrac{1}{2}at^2$, where u = 0, a = 10 m/s², s = 20:

$20 = (0 \times t) + \dfrac{1}{2}at^2 = \dfrac{10t^2}{2}$, i.e. $\underline{t = 2\text{ s}}$ when it lands (to 2 s.f.)

If its horizontal velocity is originally 5 m/s, how far has it travelled when it lands?

From above.

Using "distance = speed × time", where v = 5 and t = 2:
$s = 5 \times 2 = \underline{10\text{ m}}$.

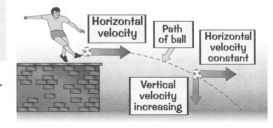

Horizontal velocity

Path of ball

Horizontal velocity constant

Vertical velocity increasing

Motion problems — Eat more figs or follow the method above...

If you follow these foolproof, step-by-step instructions to solve <u>motion</u> problems, you really can't possibly go wrong. Well, if you really try, you might be able to find a way.

Circular Motion

If it wasn't for <u>circular</u> motion our little planet would just be wandering aimlessly around the universe. And as soon as you launched a <u>satellite</u>, it'd just go flying off into space. Hardly ideal.

Circular Motion — Velocity is Constantly Changing

1) If an object is travelling in a circle it is <u>constantly</u> <u>changing direction</u>, which means it's <u>accelerating</u>.

2) This means there <u>must</u> be a <u>force</u> acting on it.

3) A force that keeps something moving in a circle is called a <u>centripetal</u> <u>force</u> — it's directed towards the <u>centre</u> of the circle.

Pronounced sen-tree-pee-tal

The velocity's in this direction, but...
...the force is always towards the centre of the circle.

Centripetal Force depends on Mass, Velocity and Radius

It's physics, so there must be an <u>equation</u>... and here it is — it's a beauty...

$$\text{Centripetal Force (N)} = \frac{\text{Mass (kg)} \times \text{Speed}^2}{\text{Radius (m)}} \qquad F = \frac{mv^2}{r}$$

1) Basically, the <u>heavier</u> the object or the <u>faster</u> it's moving, the <u>bigger</u> the centripetal force has to be to keep it moving in a <u>circle</u>.

2) And you need a <u>larger force</u> to keep something moving in a <u>smaller circle</u> (as it has 'more turning' to do).

Gravity and Electrostatic Attraction provide Centripetal Forces

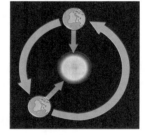

1) The <u>Earth</u> moves around the sun in an almost circular <u>orbit</u>. The centripetal force needed is provided by the <u>force of gravity</u> between the Earth and the Sun.

2) And <u>electrons</u> are kept in orbit around the <u>nucleus</u> of an atom because of <u>electrostatic attraction</u> — the <u>negative</u> charge of an electron is attracted to the <u>positive</u> charge of the nucleus in the centre of the atom.

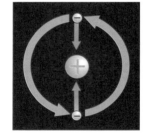

Example 1: *A 1000 kg satellite orbits the Earth at a radius of 4.23×10^7 m and a speed of 3080 m/s. Calculate the centripetal force.*

$$F = \frac{mv^2}{r} = \frac{1000 \times 3080^2}{4.23 \times 10^7} = \underline{224 \text{ N}}$$

Easy.

The Period is the Time it takes to go round Once

The <u>period</u> of an object's orbit is the <u>time</u> it takes for the object to go once round the circle.

$$\text{Period (s)} = \frac{\text{Distance travelled during orbit (m)}}{\text{Speed of Orbit (m/s)}} = \frac{2\pi r}{v}$$

This is just "velocity = distance ÷ time", using $2\pi r$ for the distance (i.e. the circumference of the orbit).

Example 2: What's the period of the above satellite's orbit?

$$\text{Period} = \frac{2\pi r}{v} = \frac{2\pi \times 4.23 \times 10^7}{3080} = \underline{86\,300 \text{ s}} \text{ (3 s.f.)}$$

I'm so dizzy — my head is spinning. It's like a whirlpool...

This is where you need to understand the difference between <u>velocity</u> and <u>speed</u> — if you think they're the same, this page will make about as much sense as a penguin up a tree. Don't be fooled into thinking that the formula for <u>orbit time</u> is something new to learn. It's just the same as <u>time = distance ÷ speed</u>.

Specific Heat Capacity & Resistors

There are a couple of other bits you might need to know about, depending on which syllabus you're doing. For example, you need to know about specific heat capacity if you're doing the OCR Physics syllabus:

Use Specific Heat Capacity to calculate Energy Transferred

There's an equation in the "heat" section of the triple-science syllabus you also need to know.
It doesn't really go with any of the stuff in the book — so we've put it here...

1) The specific heat capacity (SHC) of a material is the heat energy needed to raise the temperature of 1 kg of the stuff by 1 °C (or 1 K). (See page 71 for more about the Kelvin scale of temperature.)
2) For example, the specific heat capacity of water is 4200 J/kg/°C. This means it takes 4200 joules of heat to raise the temperature of 1 kg of water by 1 °C (or 1 kelvin).
3) You can use a material's specific heat capacity to work out how much energy has been transferred.

> Energy transferred = mass × specific heat capacity × temperature change

> *Example:* If the SHC of aluminium is 900 J/kg/°C, how much heat is required to raise the temperature of a 1.5 kg aluminium kettle by 5 °C?

> *Answer:* Energy transferred = mass × specific heat × temp. change
> = 1.5 × 900 × 5 = 6750 J

4) The higher a material's SHC, the more energy it takes to heat it up (and the more heat it can absorb without changing temperature much).
5) This is why in the old days (before fridges), food was stored in dark cupboards on shelves made from concrete or stone. Concrete has a high specific heat capacity, and so absorbs a lot of heat without changing temperature too much. This helped keep the cupboard cool and the food fresh.

And if you're doing the AQA Physics syllabus, you'll be wanting to know all about resistor colour codes...

Know how to Use the Resistor Colour Codes

Resistors have little coloured bands round them showing their resistance. You need to know how to read these resistance 'colour codes'.

1) Resistors usually have four coloured bands round them. Each colour corresponds to a value between 0 and 9.
2) The first three bands show the actual resistance of the resistor.
   (i) the first band is the first digit in the resistance,
   (ii) the second number is the second digit,
   (iii) the third digit shows the number of zeros you'd need to add to these two digits to get the actual resistance.

0	black
1	brown
2	red
3	orange
4	yellow
5	green
6	blue
7	violet
8	grey
9	white

You don't need to remember the values in this table — but you do need to know how to use them.

> *Example:* What's the resistance of the resistor on the right?
> (i) The first band is green (= 5).
> (ii) The second band is blue (= 6).
> (iii) The third band is red (so there are 2 extra zeros). So the resistance is 5600 Ω.

3) Finally, the last band is either silver or gold and shows how accurate the resistance actually is — this is called the tolerance. A gold band means the resistance is accurate to within 5%, while a silver band means it's accurate to within 10%.

> So the resistor above is accurate to within 10% — the resistance is 5600 Ω ± 10%.
> This means the actual resistance could be as little as 5600 − 560 = 5040 Ω, or it could be as big as 5600 + 560 = 6160 Ω.

No, don't be vague, what's the specific heat capacity...
That's it, then. The end of the book (almost). What are you waiting for... go pass some exams...

Revision Summary for Section Eleven

Well, here it is. You knew it was coming. The revision summary. It's like a trip to the dentist — a bit painful at the time, but for your own good in the end. Have a bash at these questions, and if there are any topics you're a bit hazy on, go back to the section and learn them. Then try those questions again, and again if you need to, until you can get them all right. And once you've done that, then I think you deserve a nice hot cup of tea and a biscuit.

1) What is the difference between elastic and plastic behaviour?
2) What is meant by the 'elastic limit' of a spring?
3) Describe how to find a spring constant.
4) How do you find the energy stored from the force/extension graph of an elastic material?
5) Describe how an elastic band acts when stretched by an increasing force.
6) What are the units of density?
7) What is the equation for density?
8) Describe how you would find the centre of mass of an irregularly shaped piece of flat cardboard.
9) Which is more stable — a low, wide object or a tall, thin one?
10) What happens if the line of action of an object's weight lies outside its base?
11) What three things can the engineer do in order to exert a larger moment on the telegraph pole?
12) Calculate the moment exerted about the nut by the force on the spanner.

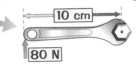

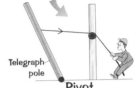

13) What must the clockwise moments be equal to for an object to balance?
14) "Momentum is usually lost in collisions and explosions." True or False?
15) An acrobat (mass 50 kg) jumps off a wall and hits the floor at a speed of 4 m/s. She bends her knees and stops moving in 0.5 s. What is the average force acting on her?
16) Explain why air bags, seat belts and crumple zones reduce the risk of serious injury in a car crash.
17) Write down the four equations of motion. Which equation should you use to find the acceleration if you know the initial velocity, the final velocity and the time taken?
18) If a bullet is fired horizontally, what happens to its horizontal and vertical velocity?
19) Explain why an object's velocity is constantly changing if it is moving in a circle.
20) What three things does a centripetal force depend on?
21) Calculate the centripetal force needed on an athletics hammer (mass 3 kg) moving in a circle of radius 1.5 m at a speed of 15 m/s. Calculate the time taken by the hammer to do a complete circle.
22) What provides the centripetal force to keep artificial satellites from drifting off into space?
23) Explain what specific heat capacity is. How much heat energy is required to increase the temperature of 3 kg of water by 7 °C? (*Take the SHC of water to be 4200 J/kg/°C.*)
24) The bands on a resistor are blue, grey, brown and gold (in that order). What are the maximum and minimum possible resistances of the resistor?

Answers

Index

Index